THE TRUTH ABOUT
ANNA
and other stories

THE TRUTH ABOUT
ANNA
and other stories

WILLIAM WARREN

ARCHIPELAGO PRESS

This compilation © William Warren 2000

First published in 2000 by Archipelago Press.

Archipelago Press is an imprint of
Editions Didier Millet (Pte) Ltd
64 Peck Seah Street
Singapore 079325

ISBN 981–3018-37–2

Printed and bound in Singapore

CONTENTS

For Tri Devakul

With many thanks

INTRODUCTION

Reading through these essays—most of which originally appeared in magazines, though often in different form—it seems to me that perhaps their only link, aside from a common Asian setting, is a taste for oddity and romance. This combination has been a personal characteristic for as long as I can remember. Even as a child, I preferred the unusual to the ordinary, the little-known to the familiar; and such inclinations remained with me as I grew up, determining what sort of books I particularly enjoyed, the places I wanted most to visit, and, after I started writing, the subjects that most appealed to me.

I was drawn to historical figures who seemed to me unjustly overlooked or misunderstood; crimes in which the perpetrator had exhibited some quirk of character—even of method—that set him or her apart; sometimes even seemingly ordinary topics that, on closer inspection, turned out to be full of unexpected details. The first article I ever wrote for an important publication (the Sunday Magazine of the *New York Times*) was about goldfish, nominally about a fad for selling pairs in plastic bags that some people regarded as inhumane. I started it without much enthusiasm until I did some research and discovered a remarkable mine of off-beat material that fascinated me. Did you know, for instance, that one of the first goldfish to reach France came as a gift from Louis XV to Madame de Pompadour, who was offended when a court wit suggested it might be a pun on her maiden name, Poisson? Or that in 1791 Prince Potemkin used bowls of the fish as part of lavish table decorations for a banquet given for

Catherine the Great in the Winter Palace? Well, I didn't; and such revelations made all the difference as far as I was concerned.

It was the same with places. While I dutifully admired such celebrated wonders as the Parthenon and the Pyramids, and understood their historical significance, I couldn't help thinking that in reality they looked exactly like the grainy black-and-white pictures in those dull books we studied in school; to me, at least, they had no resonance, no real sense of romance. Far more alluring were Chichen Itza in Yucatan with its sacrificial well, the jungle-shrouded ruins of Angkor, even the vast, strangely sinister rubber plantations of Malaysia—none of which had even been mentioned, much less shown, in those school books. Maybe because of this, I have never been much of a sightseer and have never owned a camera. Histories, anecdotes, and imagination have usually already done the job long before I actually get around to visiting a place.

All the essays collected here are the product of such tastes. They began with some odd bit of information that stimulated my curiosity, that led me on to further discoveries. Anna Leonowens, for instance, the subject of the title piece, I knew only as the sugar-sweet heroine of *The King and I*, which I saw in its first Broadway production. On the ship that brought me to Thailand when I decided to move there I read her original memoirs and discovered a somewhat different Anna, one rather less appealing but more interesting. In Bangkok I found that she was the subject of considerable controversy, for reasons that became clearer when I talked to people and read a few books of relevant Thai history. But I did not really become intrigued enough to want to write about her for another fifteen years, when new research finally revealed a totally unexpected Anna I could never have imagined when watching Gertrude Lawrence romp about the stage with a virile, bald-headed Yul Brynner.

Some of the others had a similarly long gestation period, growing out of seeds planted years before they eventually sprouted. I had a weekend house amid ruins of the old Thai capital of Ayutthaya, supposedly on the site of a palace owned by a Greek adventurer in the 17th century; how had he ended up in this remote kingdom? Thai beliefs obviously encompassed much more than Buddhism; what was the lure of all those amulets they wore around their necks, those shrines I could see all around me in Bangkok? That little magical island I saw off the southern coast of Sri Lanka, with the strange house on top—who had created it, and why?

The answers sometimes lay buried in old memoirs and travel books, or in academic studies not aimed at the general reader, or in faded newspapers and magazines gathering dust on a library shelf. I can claim credit for few, if any, original discoveries; the research was done by others, sometimes long ago, and all I did was rescue it from what seemed to me undeserved oblivion.

In this process I have been fortunate to write for a number of editors on such publications as *Asia* (the magazine of the Asia Society), *The Reader's Digest*, *Winds* (the inflight magazine of Japan Air Lines) and the *New York Times*, who have shared my curiosities and supported me in pursuing them. I am deeply grateful to all of them.

Bangkok, 2000

1

THE TRUTH ABOUT ANNA

Almost as soon as I came to live in Thailand, in 1960, an English resident offered me a piece of helpful advice. "Don't mention Anna and the King," he said. "It makes the Thais furious."

I found this to be true enough, at least among those Thais who had travelled abroad during the previous decade. The immensely successful Broadway musical *The King and I* and the Hollywood film version had brought to a boil resentments that had been simmering ever since 1944 when Margaret Landon rescued Anna from oblivion with the publication of her best-selling *Anna and the King of Siam*.

That book, like the two nineteenth-century works by Anna Leonowens on which it was based—*The English Governess at the Court of Siam* and *The Romance of the Harem*—had gravely offended Thais who read it, but their number was comparatively small. Similarly, an earlier, non-musical movie made from Mrs. Landon's book with Irene Dunne as Anna and Rex Harrison as a very suave king had not caused much of a commotion.

The King and I, though, was a different matter. Not only was it spreading the controversial old story to an audience of millions all over the world, it was also presenting what most Thais regarded as a gross caricature of a revered ruler, who was depicted as a half-naked savage who sang comic patter songs and swooped up Gertrude Lawrence (on stage) and Deborah Kerr (on film) to dance a spirited polka through the hallowed halls of the Grand Palace. It was as if Abraham Lincoln had been presented doing a tap dance while reading the Emancipation Proclamation, the idea for which he got from a White House intern.

After screening the film, the Thai government banned it as an insult to the monarchy and a possible encouragement to Communist subversion.

The rest of the world, though, seemed enchanted with the tale of the plucky young English governess and the autocratic monarch. Taking Anna's version, further embellished by Mrs. Landon, on faith, most Westerners credited her with nothing less than the moral enlightenment of the Thai royal family, which she achieved through personal example and by tactfully imparting Christian ideals. Typical of the tributes paid to her were the stirring words of Dame Freya Stark, the noted Middle Eastern traveller, who wrote an introduction to a new, 1952 edition of *The Romance of the Harem*: "Harassed and indomitable, she loved the women in their royal slavery and trained a new and happier generation of children to carry light into the future; and few people can have wielded a stronger influence in that corner of Asia."

In the face of such enthusiasm, it is perhaps not surprising that the Thai protests went largely ignored. Only later did historians, Western as well as Thai, begin to seriously probe Anna's legend, and what they have come up with is scarcely calculated to please her admirers.

* * * * *

To begin with, it was fairly easy to demonstrate that both her books—particularly the second one—are strewn with obvious errors and distortions. Anna claims, for example, to have learned the Siamese language; but with all possible allowances made for clumsy transliterations, most of the example she offers are incomprehensible. One must question, therefore, her professed ability to chat at length with the ladies of the harem and to record the sensational stories allegedly learned from them.

Anna lived in Bangkok from 1862 to 1867, working for a ruler who was passionately interested in the history of his kingdom, yet she never learned the proper name of the Chao Phraya River that flows through the city. Like most other Westerners of the time, she makes the mistake of calling it the Meinam, which simply means "large river". She calls Chiang Mai "the capital of Laos country"; says Ayutthaya was destroyed by the Burmese around 1632 (more than a century before the actual date); and confuses King Taksin, the founder of Thonburi, with Rama I, the founder of Bangkok. Her passages on Buddhism are either confused (she never understood the role of Brahmanic rituals in royal ceremony) or shamelessly plagiarized from other writers, and she includes a detailed account of a journey she never made to Angkor Wat (she lifted it, sometimes word for word, from the published journal of Henri Mouhot, which came out around the time she was writing *The English Governess*).

Her worst errors occur in *The Romance of the Harem*, when, in the words of one critic, "her store of pertinent facts was running low". In this she claims the king threw wives who displeased him into underground dungeons below the Grand Palace and that he ordered the sacrifice and burial of a number of innocent people under a new gate built in the palace wall in 1865. Her most horrific tale describes, in vivid detail, the royally decreed public torture and burning of a consort and her lover, a Buddhist monk. Anna says she was "an unwilling witness" to most of this dreadful spectacle, near the end of which "I was completely exhausted and worn out, and had no strength left to endure further sight of this monstrous, this inhuman tragedy. Kind nature came to my relief, and I fainted".

None of this is true, or if it is it managed to escape the notice of every other foreign resident of Bangkok, including the eagle-eyed

Dr. Dan Beach Bradley, an American missionary who befriended Anna and kept a detailed journal. There were no dungeons in the Grand Palace, or anywhere else in Bangkok. As the historian Alexander Griswold notes, "It is even now a formidable task to build any sort of underground room in that watery soil; before the days of reinforced concrete it was an impossibility." As for the king's attitude toward his women, there is a record of one having been abducted; the man was let off with a fine amounting to about six dollars. Griswold thinks Anna got the idea for her horror story from a "silly bit of doggerel" quoted in a book by an earlier English resident who vaguely claimed it was "a lament supposed to be uttered by a guilty priest, previous to his suffering along with the partner of his guilt the dreadful punishment attached to his transgression". The last stanza of the lament reads as follows:

Behold the faggots blaze up high
    The smoke is black and dense;
The sinews burst, and crack, and fly:
    Of suffering intense!

The roar of fire and shriek of pain,
    And the blood that boils and splashes,
These all consume—the search were vain
    For the lovers' mingled ashes.

To Thais, Anna's most unforgiveable sin was the portrait she painted of her royal employer, King Mongkut (Rama IV). While praising him here and there for his intelligence and devotion to duty, she seems more concerned with presenting him as a sadistic, lustful tyrant. She calls him "revolting", "envious, revengeful, subtle, and cruel", and "a barbarian and a despot". In summation, she says,

"Considered apart from his domestic relations, he was, in many respects, an able and virtuous ruler . . . But as husband and kinsman his character assumes a most revolting aspect."

This is scarcely the man revealed by every other history book or in the journals of other foreigners who met him. Mongkut was 58 years old and had been on the throne for 11 years at the time of Anna's arrival. Before that, he had spent 26 years as a Buddhist monk, a period that had shaped him intellectually as no Thai king had ever been before. Freed by his yellow robe from the medieval rituals and restraints of palace life, he had travelled extensively about the country, meeting ordinary people and learning about their daily life. He had also formed friendships with a number of Christian missionaries, both Catholic and Protestant, and gained knowledge of comparative religion, astronomy, mathematics, history, and such foreign languages as English, French, and Latin. As abbot of a prominent Bangkok temple, he launched a determined effort to purge Thai Buddhism of various superstitions that had crept in over the centuries; and if he was not wholly successful he at least set standards that are still felt today.

Long before he was selected by the royal council to succeed his half-brother as king in 1851 (and even longer before he met Anna), he had developed an open-mindedness remarkable for a man of his age and rank, as well as a determination to reform and modernize his kingdom. He set about the latter task with a notable energy almost at once. Innovative edicts poured from the palace on almost every aspect of Thai life, however mundane—on the proper construction of ovens to avoid fires, on religious tolerance, on the selection of judges, on "the inelegant practice of throwing dead animals into the waterways". Previous kings had been reluctant to give up royal trade monopolies, and foreign missions seeking a more enlightened policy had met with little success. Mongkut, on the other hand, warmly welcomed Sir John Bowring in 1855 and in the space of a few months reached agreement on a historic diplomatic and commercial treaty with Great Britain. (Bowring, incidentally, devoted several pages of his account to the king's obvious love of his children.)

Nothing better illustrates his personal tolerance than his relationship with Dr. Dan Beach Bradley, who published a newspaper (Thailand's first) in which he openly attacked the "pernicious custom" of royal polygamy. Any of Mongkut's predecessors would almost certainly have expelled the doctor for *lèse-majeste*. Mongkut, though, who respected Bradley for his medical work as well as for his honesty, merely wrote a letter explaining the custom in relation to the country's customs, religion, and politics. In 1854, he went further by issuing a decree that allowed the palace women to resign if they were dissatisfied with their lot; only twelve did so, and none of them suffered any consequences as a result.

Mongkut's harem was undeniably a large one and, as if to make up for lost time, he managed to have a total of 81 children by 27 wives—the largest number achieved by any of his dynasty. To his subjects, if not to Dr. Bradley, this was wholly admirable, proof not only of his virility but also ensuring a wide choice of candidates when it came time to choose the next ruler.

Typical, too, was his decision to provide a broader education for some of his wives and his children. He tried at first bringing in three of the missionary women (including Mrs. Bradley), but though it continued for almost three years this proved unsatisfactory; the ladies insisted on combining language instruction with religious propagation, not at all what Mongkut had in mind. He eventually applied for help to his Singapore agent, who in turn suggested Anna. The king's letter confirming the appointment is a fair example of his eccentric English (about the only aspect of *The King and I* that has some validity), as well as of his personality:

English Era, 1862, 26th February
Grand Royal Palace, Bangkok

To Mrs. A.H. Leonowens:

MADAM: We are in good pleasure, and satisfaction in heart, that you are in willingness to undertake the education of our beloved royal children. And we hope that in doing your education on us and on our children (whom English call inhabitants of benighted land) you will do your best endeavor for knowledge of English language, science, and literature, and not for conversion to Christianity; as the followers of Buddha are mostly aware of the powerfulness of truth and virtue, as well as the followers of Christ, and are desirous to have facility of English language and literature, more than new religions.

We beg to invite you to our royal palace to do your best endeavorment upon us and our children. We shall expect to see you here on return of Siamese steamer Chow Phya.

We have written to Mr. William Adamson, and to our consul in Singapore, to authorize to do best arrangement for you and ourselves.

Believe me.

Your faithfully,
(Signed)
S.S.P.P. Maha Mongut

(Note that there is no mention of the term "governess"; she was hired simply as a teacher.)

In 1868, a year after Anna left Bangkok, Mongkut contracted a fatal case of malaria while on a trip to view a total solar eclipse that he had accurately predicted. Thus he never read either *The English Governess at the Court of Siam* or *The Romance of the Harem*. One wonders what he would have made of them. Would he have gone into a rage (for he did, by most accounts, have a short temper)? Exhibited the sort of tolerance he had over Dr. Bradley's views of polygamy? Or, perhaps, merely felt an acute sense of puzzlement?

* * * * *

Anna's two memoirs, especially the first, enjoyed a measure of success when they appeared in the United States and Great Britain, but only a few Thais seem to have read them. One was the scholarly Prince Damrong, one of Mongkut's sons, who took a charitable view; when asked about them in 1930 by an English friend, he commented, "Mrs. Leonowens added drama to her story in order to make money from her books for the support of her children. As a governess, she carried far less influence with the king than she said. After all, she was only a governess but she was tempted to make out she had said many things which in retrospect she may have wished she had said."

In any event, the books were long out of print and largely forgotten when Margaret Landon, a former missionary, came upon them shortly before the Second World War. Combining the two she came up with *Anna and the King of Siam*, which she claimed was only lightly fictionalized but essentially true. She also included a chapter of biographical material on her heroine's background, which she undoubtedly believed to be accurate since it came from Anna's granddaughter who in turn had gotten it from Anna herself. It was this chapter that later provided the clues which led to the most surprising revelations.

None of the historians who did such a thorough demolition job on Anna's account of her Thai experiences seemed inclined to look further. They accepted her (and Margaret Landon's) version of her pre-Bangkok life, which may be summarized as follows.

She was born, she said, at Caernarvon in Wales, in 1834, which would have made her twenty-eight when she arrived to take up her position in King Mongkut's court. Her mother, Selina Edwards, came from an old Welsh family and her father, Thomas Maxwell Crawford, was a captain in the army. When Anna was six she and an older sister were left behind when her parents went to India, where not long afterwards Captain Crawford was hacked to pieces during a Sikh uprising in Lahore.

After completing her education at fourteen or fifteen, Anna and her sister sailed for India and an unpleasant surprise. In the words of Dame Freya Stark, "She found her mother married to a stepfather so uncongenial that she was rarely heard to mention his name in after life." One reason for her intense dislike was that he wanted to marry her off to a wealthy merchant more than twice her age, while Anna had fallen in love with a handsome young officer named Thomas Leonowens. To escape the situation, she went off on a lengthy tour of the Middle East with a well-known traveller named Reverend George Percy Badger and his wife, who were presumably friends of the family.

"Under the influence of this distinguished Orientalist," writes Dame Freya, "she studied Arabic and engaged a Persian munshi who was to attend her for many years. Her vision of Asia was widened in a manner impossible in an India verging on the Mutiny; and she returned to her family after nearly a year's absence, with a character already strongly formed, both for tolerance and independence."

She was independent enough to defy her stepfather and elope at the tender age of seventeen with her young officer, who, Dame Freya assures us, "turned out to a be a devoted, affectionate, and faithful husband". The couple started out grandly, living on fashionable Malabar Hill in Bombay (now Mumbai) with numerous servants, but tragedy soon struck with a series of heavy blows. In one year, 1852, both Anna's mother and her first child, a daughter, died; when the couple sailed for England on a trip to assuage her grief, their ship was wrecked near the Cape of Good Hope and they were picked up by another vessel bound for Australia; there a second child died before they were finally able to continue their journey to what they hoped would be better fortune.

In England, things briefly improved. They lived in the smart St. James's district of London and were blessed with two more children: Avis, born in 1854, and Louis, a year later. In 1857 Leonowens, by then promoted to Major, rejoined his regiment in Singapore and it was there that Anna received the news that a small fortune left to her by her father had been lost with the collapse of a bank in Agra during the Indian Mutiny. A year later, Major Leonowens suffered sunstroke on a tiger hunt and died, leaving Anna with two small children and no money.

Friends rallied round to help and she began a school for officers' children, bringing in enough to enable her to send Avis back to relatives in England but not much more. A new challenge came with the offer to go to Siam, and with characteristic courage off she went, accompanied by young Louis and the munshi she had acquired on her trip with the Badgers.

This was the "Mrs. Anna" of Margaret Landon's book, of all the gracious ladies who have portrayed her on stage and screen: a refined but plucky gentlewoman who had known both joy and sadness, bravely venturing forth to bring her civilized ways to a barbaric kingdom. (She bore, at least one writer has perceptively observed, a remarkable resemblence to Mrs. Landon, who seems to have closely identified herself with her heroine.)

Except for the detested stepfather and the trip to the Middle East, almost every detail of this touching story is as false as her account of the terrible burning of the young consort and her priestly lover.

Credit for discovering most of the truth belongs to Dr. W.S. Bristowe, a frequent visitor to Bangkok from England. Dr. Bristowe's usual subject was spiders, on which he was a noted expert, but he also wrote on other topics. He had long been interested in Louis

Leonowens, Anna's son, who had returned to Thailand as a young man and enjoyed a colourful career, pioneering in the northern teak industry and starting a company that still bears his name. He seemed a promising subject for a biography, and in the early 1970s Dr. Bristowe set about collecting material for one.

To ascertain the exact date of Louis' birth in London, he made a routine check of the records. At once he ran into a mystery: neither the birth of Louis or Avis was recorded. Nor, when he looked further, could he find any record of anyone named Thomas Leonowens who had served in the British army in either India or England. Nor did the army know anything about the man Anna claimed to be her distinguished father. Strangest of all, archives in Wales failed to provide any mention of Anna herself.

By now, Dr. Bristowe's curiosity was thoroughly aroused, and he set about tracking the elusive Anna with all the enthusiasm he normally gave to a rare species of spider. Diligent research eventually yielded the following story, which he reported in his book, perhaps inevitably called *Louis and the King of Siam*.

* * * * *

Anna was born not in Wales but in India, and not in 1834 but in 1831. Her father was Thomas Edwards, a cabinetmaker from Middlesex who enlisted in the Bombay Infantry and went to the subcontinent in 1825. There he married Mary Anne Glasscock, who, far from being of noble lineage, probably had either an Indian or a Eurasian mother. The couple had two daughters, Eliza and Anna, and Edwards died three months before the birth of the latter, leaving his widow almost nothing and certainly no small fortune for Anna to lose in the Mutiny.

When Anna was two months old, her mother remarried, this time to a corporal (soon demoted to private for some unknown offence).

Dr. Bristowe believes that Anna and Eliza were sent to England for a time with their father's relatives, probably through the aid of a charity. They returned in their early teens to a home that "must have appalled them", for the life of a private soldier in India at the time was one of squalor, in which "drunkenness and fornication were the principal occupations".

Eliza was married off at fifteen to a sergeant in the horse artillery. Something similar was no doubt planned for Anna—this one of the few points where her story and the truth coincide—but she went off instead to the Middle East with the Reverend Mr. Badger, when she was fourteen and he was thirty. He was not, however, married, and their tour may not have been character-building in quite the way Dame Freya Stark thought. (Another researcher, it should be noted here, feels nothing untoward happened on the long journey, citing the fact that Badger was one of the few people from her early life of whom Anna always spoke with affection and gratitude.)

Anna's own marriage came when she was eighteen. It was not to a dashing officer but to a lowly clerk, and his name was not Leonowens but Thomas Leon Owens. He never held any job for long, and the couple was constantly on the move. Dr. Bristowe never did succeed in pinning down the births of Louis and Avis, concluding finally that they must have taken place in Australia or possibly on board a ship. At some other unknown point, Leon Owens became Leonowens, and Dr. Bristowe did find a record of his death—of apoplexy, in Penang, where he was listed as a "hotel master".

Susan Fulop Kepner, a teacher at the University of California in Berkeley, has added other details and conjecture to this history. A well-known scholar of things Thai and the translator of several modern Thai novels, Ms. Kepner writes from a feminist point of view and is reported to be working on a joint biography of Anna and Margaret Landon. She finds Dr. Bristowe's account "unrelievedly mean-spirited" but apparently accepts most of his findings and adds a few of her own, gleaned from a perusal of Mrs. Landon's papers.

On the matter of Anna's racial background, for example—what Dr. Bristowe calls her having "a touch of the tar brush"—she discovered that more than one person had commented on her "exotic" appearance in later life. One, who had known her long after she left Bangkok, wrote Mrs. Landon that, "We all thought [her dark appearance] must be a consequence of the Siamese sun." She also found a curious letter written by a grandson of Anna's sister Eliza to Anna's daughter Avis, in which he said that Eliza had happened to meet a seaman who had encountered Anna in Bangkok. Since the two had lost contact, Eliza wrote her sister; in return she received a "very strange reply", in which Anna said she wanted to cut off all communication with her relations and that if any of them came to Siam to find her "she would commit suicide".

Ms. Kepner also indulges in some lurid speculation. A possible explanation for Anna's intense hatred of her stepfather, she suggests, may have been sexual as well as physical abuse, and that her trip with the Reverend Badger could have been "the traditional standard journey taken by unmarried young women about to display evidence of impending motherhood".

* * * * *

With such a background it is scarcely surprising that when she received the opportunity to start a new life in Bangkok, Anna decided to wipe the slate clean and invent an entirely new persona. She did this so sucessfully that neither of her children ever knew the truth. (Nor, perhaps, did Anna ever know that one of Eliza's daughters married a prosperous Eurasian named Pratt or that the youngest child of this union later became the actor Boris Karloff of

Frankenstein movie fame.)

Initially, she may not have been as skilled as the various actresses who portrayed her. The foreign community of Bangkok was small in those days, rather rigidly divided into consular staff, merchants, seamen, and missionaries. Anna was never taken up by the first group, despite her position at court, perhaps because she waited nine days before calling at the British Consulate—a major breach of etiquette—more likely because she was unable to sustain her pose of respectability around its well-born members. The merchants were not much more hospitable, even the manager of the Borneo Company who had sponsored her selection; and the seamen, on the whole, were a rough, hard-drinking crowd she would have avoided (though one of them, the captain of the ship that brought her to Bangkok, proposed marriage to her and was still pressing his suit after she left Siam). That left the Protestant missionaries, including Dr. Bradley, who would be less likely to notice any social gaffes or to question the cultured background she pretended to have.

They gave her the friendship and support she needed so badly. Dr. Bradley in particular seems to have become close to her. Although he noted in a memoir, "I could have wished . . . that she had appeared more frequently at church on Sunday," she loyally supported him in a libel suit filed by the French Consul General for an article in the *Bangkok Recorder* and corresponded with him after she left Siam; one letter, written from Staten Island, New York, in 1870, mentions that she has published sketches about her experiences in the *Atlantic* magazine and closes with the words "Bangkok is the most hideous word I have ever written or uttered".

In return for this friendship, though, she had to adopt their narrow-minded prejudices about religion and polygamy, which helped shape her views of King Mongkut and his court. The inventions and distortions in her books may be have been partly designed to boost sales, but they were also aimed at convincing Dr. Bradley and company that Anna Leonowens was truly a virtuous Christian woman.

Anna's subsequent life was outwardly a happy one, whatever inner demons may have tormented her. After spending several years in the United States (where both her books were written) she settled with her daughter Avis in Nova Scotia. There she became active in feminist causes, especially women's suffrage, and gained a wide circle of admirers; there, too, she died in 1916 at the ripe old age of eighty-five (not eighty-two, as her friends and family thought), still playing, with by now accomplished ease, a role that might have daunted her later impersonators.

Meanwhile, the myth continues to enjoy a vigorous life. *The King and I* is nearly always being presented somewhere in the world—once more on Broadway a few years ago—and Hollywood has returned to the non-musical Margaret Landon romance with Jodie Foster as the noble heroine. Permission was sought to film in Bangkok, but after studying the script the authorities, not surprisingly, declined to grant it; the production was shot instead in Malaysia, using an expensive re-creation of the Grand Palace.

A unique opportunity may have been missed, and not just in the setting. Instead of repeating the bland, peaches-and-cream character seen so often before, surely an actress of Jodie Foster's range and intelligence would have preferred to attempt an interpretation of the real Anna—brave beyond any doubt, but also shrewd and more than a little neurotic, driven by forces that might have destroyed a lesser woman.

2

THE ROMANCE OF ASIAN TRAVEL

Once, on a flight from Bangkok to Singapore, I happened to sit next to an American businessman who was on a quick, professional trip through the region. It was the first time he had been to Asia, he told me, and so naturally I asked him what he thought of the various cities he had visited.

But his answers depressed me. As far as I could gather, his impressions were gathered almost entirely from the hotels he had stayed in; and since most of these had been standard, international establishments, uniform in their comforts and design, the cities, too, had struck him as all but indistinguishable. Tokyo was in Japan, Bangkok in Thailand, the people spoke a different language; otherwise he seemed to find little difference between the two. Nor, as he passed over the Straits of Malacca, did he appear particularly intrigued by the prospect of Singapore just ahead.

Such a bland approach to travel is, I suppose, not all that unusual considering the vast number of people moving about the world these days, but it never fails to surprise and faintly shock me. It is so completely contrary to my own sensations; for even after nearly fifty years of regular exposure to exotic places I can still never board a plane or train without a tingle of pleasurable anticipation, a magical sense of adventure in the offing.

I was raised on travel literature that stressed the sheer romance of strange places, and the effects have never left me. As a child I relished the marvellous adventure books of Richard Halliburton (does anyone read Halliburton nowadays?), with their evocative descriptions of midnight visits to the Taj Mahal, a dive into the sacred well at Chichen Itza, a swim across the Bosphorus. I hoarded stacks of well-thumbed National Geographic magazines, returning again and again to those lush photographs of Bali and Bombay (Mumbai), Komodo dragons and Kandyan drum dancers.

Later, I graduated to the atmospheric stories of Maugham and Kipling, then to the travel accounts of such intrepid wanderers as Stanley and Burton and Dame Freya Stark (who crossed the Arabian desert with a band of Bedouins). Long before I had ventured very far from the city limits of the small town where I was born, I had accumulated a sizeable mental library of vivid images, ranging from the arctic wastes of the South Pole to the steamy jungles of Borneo, and it is one I continually find myself drawing on to this day.

Just the names of places, to begin with, carry a heavy freight of tantalizing connotations, often potent enough to overcome the disillusionment of reality. "Names have a life of their own," wrote that canny old traveller Somerset Maugham, "and though Trebizond may be nothing but a poverty-stricken village the glamour of its name must invest it for all right-thinking minds with the trappings of Empire; and Samarkand: can anyone write the word without a quickening of the pulse and at his heart the pain of unsatisfied desire? . . . The streets of Mandalay, dusty, crowded, and drenched with a garish sun, are broad and straight. Tram cars lumber down them with a rout of passengers; they fill the seats and gangways and cling thickly to the footboard like flies clustered upon an over-ripe mango. The houses, with their balconies and verandahs, have the slatternly look of houses in the Main Street of a Western town that has fallen on evil days . . . It does not matter: Mandalay has its name; the falling cadence of that lovely word has gathered about itself the chiaroscuro of romance."

Ho Chi Minh City, Thailand, Kampuchea, Sri Lanka, Myanmar.

The names undoubtedly represent something important to the patriots who devised them. They may well reflect modern realities better than the old ones that used to appear on the maps I studied so avidly long ago. But for me at least they can never have the allure of Saigon and Siam, Cambodia, Ceylon, Burma, names encrusted with magic and mystery like the patina that covers a fine old piece of bronze. Jim Thompson, the man who started the famous Thai silk industry, felt the same way; when I first met him I remember being surprised at the way he invariably used "Siam" and "Siamese" in talking about the country he had adopted as his home, even though the official name had been changed some years before. "It was Siam when I first knew it," he told me when I asked, "and I will always think of it as Siam. Such a lovely, exotic word; I hate to give it up."

(Sometimes, if you wait long enough, the old names come back. Kampuchea reverted to Cambodia in due course; and Burma, at least to the *New York Times*, has never become Myanmar. Others have stubbornly endured in spite of changes. When King Rama I decided to relocate the Thai capital to a small trading center on the Chao Phraya River called Bangkok, he invested it with a long, impressive title which appears on Thai-language maps in the abbreviated form of Krung Thep, loosely translatable as "City of Angels." But "Bangkok" had already entered the world's vocabulary thanks to earlier travellers and refused to be replaced—perhaps because it sounded so right with its suggestion of temple gongs and strangely dissonant melodies. Who, after all, could imagine Noel Coward's celebrated lyrics being changed to read "In Krung Thep/At twelve o'clock/They foam at the mouth and run . . ."?)

And think of the others: Manila, a sound as languid as the breezes that sweep across its bay; Singapore, evoking both Empire and Orient; the sonorous chimes of Rangoon; the smoky beauty of Shanghai. And Kathmandu, Kuching, Kota Kinabalu, the matchless rhythm of Hong Kong. Unseen, unexperienced, they already have the power to stir a romantic imagination.

"We have just landed in Kuching. Please keep your seat belts fastened until the plane has come to a complete stop at the terminal building." Kuching! A leisurely little place, somnolent even; you can cover most of it on foot in a few hours. My unromantic businessman would probably pronounce it a bore and get out as fast as possible.

Not I. My mental library has already surrounded it with an aura so tangible that I am bewitched even before I disembark. Here the White Rajahs ruled from their eccentric istana on the broad, brown river, and though the last of them departed in 1946 their ghosts are vividly present for me as I stroll along the arcaded sidewalks of Kuching.

The first Rajah was the swashbuckler, fighting pirates and headhunters and carving a kingdom out of the inhospitable jungles of Borneo (Sarawak). He was also, unfortunately, impotent, a fact that caused Errol Flynn to abandon plans to star in a film based on his adventurous life; Flynn, it seems, insisted on a love interest. The second Rajah wore a false eye intended for a stuffed albatross, and every morning, dressed in a blue serge coat and white trousers, with a sprig of honeysuckle in his buttonhole, sat in judgment in the elegant old courthouse that still stands beside the river. His decisions, says one account, were based on "customary law, the code of British India, and common sense"; dismissing a complaint against a young couple found making love on a pile of timber, he went straight to the heart of the matter, asking "Was there any damage to the wood?" The last Rajah was a man Flynn would have admired: he was still attracting young ladies when he was in his eighties (to the affectionate dismay of his wife), and during the war the conquering Japanese papered the walls of his office with old love letters.

With ghosts like these, how could anyone find Kuching dull? Not to mention the great Borneo jungle that lurks just outside, with orangutans, hornbills, *Rafflesia arnoldii*, the largest flower in the world (leafless, stemless, a metre or more in diameter, and smelling like rotten meat), and Dayak in their incredible longhouses, many hung with bunches of yellowing old skulls.

Not a fair example, I can hear my businessman protesting: much too exotic. Progress, after all, has touched Kuching but lightly with its heavy, unsentimental hand, leaving most of the Rajah's quaint architectural follies more or less unscathed. It doesn't require all that much effort to be romantic when the setting is so right.

But what of a place like Tokyo, built almost entirely on the ashes of the old? What of Bangkok, where the fairy-tale temples and palaces of Rama I must compete with horrendous traffic and endless miles of charmless row-shops? What of Hong Kong with its feverish, never-ending building boom, of Singapore's constantly changing skyline, of all the other cities where war or progress (or both) have removed most of the visible vestiges of the legendary past?

Once again Maugham offers a text worth pondering. "There are people," he notes in one of his stories, "who take salt in their coffee. They say it gives it a tang, a savour, which is peculiar and fascinating. In the same way there are certain places, surrounded by a halo of romance, to which the inevitable disillusionment which you must experience on seeing them gives a singular spice. You had expected something wholly beautiful, and you get an impression which is infinitely more complicated than any beauty can give you. It is like the weakness in the character of a great man which makes him less admirable but certainly makes him more interesting."

Maugham was inspired to these comments by his first visit to Honolulu (of which he goes on to say, "though the air is so soft and the sky so blue, you have, I know not why, a feeling of something hotly passionate that beats like a throbbing pulse through the crowd"), but I think they also apply to other fabled cities in Asia where preconceptions clash violently with first impressions.

The unimaginative traveller is often defeated with bewildering speed in such places. The few frail images he has brought from *Shogun* and *The King and I* collapse like sand castles before the sassy swagger of Tokyo's Ginza, the erotic discos of Bangkok's Patpong Road. Unwilling to risk further disenchantment, he retreats to the safe comforts of his familiar hotel, which is perhaps holding "Italian Week" complete with a butter sculpture of the Coliseum.

Others, though, addicted by the pure romance of travel, find the complexity, the contradictions, all the more exciting. The cities are already steeped in glamor for us, they have become a part of ourselves, reaching far back into our childhood dreams; no amount of superficial change can rob them of their magic, for we can never view them with the clear, sober eye of objectivity.

So what if the Victorian charm of Hong Kong's old waterfront has been largely replaced by towers of glass and cement? If the famous Star Ferry to Kowloon has been rendered redundant by the engineering marvel of the harbour tunnel? For us romantics, it remains the Hong Kong of legend, with its breathtaking views of peak and port, its snaking, clamourous alleyways, its lingering blend of British reserve and rakish buccaneer. Not for a minute could we mistake it for Singapore, a sedate old dowager looking through her lorgnette with faint disaste at the shenanigans of less orderly societies.

Even Tokyo, that sprawling Phoenix of a city that has risen again and again from fire and earthquake, never fails to delight us with its odd juxtapositions: the garish pachinko parlour next to the lantern-lit courtyard, the kimono-clad ladies in supermarkets, the television set on the tatami mat. While other, more conventional visitors take special courses in the intricacies of the tea ceremony and search desperately for surviving relics of Lafcadio Hearn, we relish the most bizarre, futuristic aspects, which almost invariably are given a delicate twist, a subtle shading, that makes them somehow uniquely Japanese.

I still remember the musical coffee shops, for instance, which were all the rage some years ago. One I went to occupied four or five different levels, all built around a central well in which a string quartet on an elevator went slowly up and down, playing classical music. Nor can I ever forget the mind-boggling shows that used to be staged at the Nichigeki Music Hall—in one a Chinese junk sank in a terrifying storm, while a full symphony orchestra played Ravel's *Bolero* and half-clad chorus girls undulated on raised platforms along the walls. At the peak of this spectacle the foreign friend I was with murmured reverently, "My God. Where else would you see a sight like this?" Where else indeed?

And where else can one see such an imaginative use of neon, transforming the narrow, nondescript streets of Shinjuku into enchanted grottos each night? Or such marvellous department stores, where one can move from the latest in electronic gadgets to an exhibition of sixteenth-century kimonos? Or such a successful blend of big-city excitement and close-knit, self-contained neighbourhoods, each with its own particular flavour?

These are the qualities that make Tokyo special to me: a long way from Lafcadio, perhaps, but an even longer way from London and New York.

Nor does actually living in a legendary place, growing gradually to regard it as home, breed complacency in a diehard romantic. I have been a resident of Bangkok for more than half my life, its sights and sounds and smells are as familiar to me as those of the American town where I grew up; yet I never cease to be aware of its wonderful strangeness, the discoveries that lie in wait everywhere.

As I write this, the neighbourhood noodle vendor is pedalling his ponderous mobile kitchen down the street just outside, sounding his Harpo Marx bulb horn to lure anyone who wants an instant meal. Last week an elephant looked over my gate; its mahout had brought it down from near the Cambodian border to earn some money from city dwellers who want to walk under its belly and thereby gain good luck. Not far from where I live there is a restaurant that sells cobra meat and has a tank of live snakes to choose from. When I go into town to my bank, I pass a popular shrine that always offers some sight of unusual interest to relieve the tedium of a traffic snarl—a troop of Thai classical dancers, perhaps, or a human pyramid formed by professional acrobats, presented in gratitude to the resident spirit for favours granted.

Or, if I want, I can wander through the amulet market and perhaps find a small clay votive tablet that will protect me from snakebite, bullets, and a broken heart; go to a museum devoted to white elephants and see the preserved skin of one that died in 1856; sit in a reclining chair across from the Temple of the Emerald Buddha and view a kite fight; or eat a bowl of curry overlooking the broad river with its endless processions of rice barges coming down from the countryside, just as Joseph Conrad did a century ago.

Bangkok may be home; but it is still, above all, Bangkok.

"The good traveller," wrote Maugham, "has the gift of surprise." So, I think, does the real romantic, always approaching each new experience with a thrill of anticipation, sometimes perhaps expecting too much, but never for a moment in any danger of regarding travel as routine.

3

WRITERS WHO CREATED ROMANCE

The year was 1926, the place an auditorium in Pasadena, California. The boyish-looking young man surveyed his audience of complacent, middle-class citizens and then launched into a most subversive lecture: "Don't be steady, women. Don't be steady, men. God made the world so large for restless people that when you feel that urge to be off on the Royal Road to Romance, rebel against the prosaic mould into which you are being poured and fare forth in search of the beautiful, the joyous, and the romantic."

The young man's name was Richard Halliburton, and he was promoting his first book, an account of personal adventures in remote places called, of course, *The Royal Road to Romance*.

It was not, in fact, a very good book. The author used a gushy, gee-whiz style to describe such experiences as bathing nude by moonlight in the pool of the Taj Mahal ("It was a taste of paradise"), and few critics had kind words for it. But over the years it sold more than a million copies and launched Halliburton on a notable career as a travel writer that ended only when he vanished somewhere in the Pacific in 1939, while trying to sail a Chinese junk from Hong Kong to San Francisco.

The reasons for its success are implicit in the title. In those not-really-so-long-ago years before mass air travel, remote places were almost synonymous with romance; and since comparatively few people had the courage or the means to visit them in reality, they were eager to do so vicariously, through the medium of the printed page.

Writers—some of the Halliburton school, others of genius—were their guides, laying the foundation for romantic legends that still lurk in the sensibilities of their jet-age grandchildren, though they may not always realize it.

This was particularly true of that exotic region that lay, in Kipling's magical phrase, "East of Suez". As one historian put it, "A scent of incense, spice, perfumed woman, sandalwood and opium drifted from the Orient to the Occident"; and, in large part, the scent was the creation of literary wanderers who fed the romance-hungry imaginations of countless millions back home.

The process began as long ago as Marco Polo, whose thirteenth-century tales of life in the court of the Great Khan stirred day-dreams across much of Europe. Some modern historians doubt Marco Polo ever went to China, and several recent books have been devoted to the matter. No matter: true or not, the stories were told, the impact was made. Consider, for instance, his account of how additions were made to the ruler's harem. Candidates were ranked like jewels, he says, "and if the Great Khan has ordered that those to be brought to him should be of 20 or 21 carats, the required number of that value is brought to him." These are then reappraised and thinned out to the thirty or forty of the highest quality.

"Then he has one given to each of the wives of his barons, to have them sleep in the same bed with them, and see carefully whether they are virgins, and perfectly healthy under every point of view, whether they have a quiet sleep or else snore, whether their breath is good and sweet, or else evil, and whether they in any way have an unpleasant odour. When they have been thus diligently examined, those that are found to be beautiful and good and sound under every aspect, are appointed to wait on the Lord."

What heady reading that must have made in far-away Italy, only just emerging from the bleak Middle Ages!

Ensuing centuries brought more traders and explorers to the mysterious East, and their discoveries, too, struck resonant chords. Although the validity of Fernao Mendes Pinto's account of his wanderings in the sixteenth century is as controversial as that of Marco Polo's, he nevertheless produced a classic of Portuguese literature in the *Peregrination*, written after his return.

He claimed to have visited the great Siamese capital of Ayutthaya and offered one of the first glimpses of that fabulous animal the White Elephant, which he saw being taken to the river to bathe. "He was shaded from the sun by twenty-four servants carrying white parasols. His guard numbered three thousand men. It was like a procession on a day of festival. Before and behind him were about thirty lords on elephants. He had a chain of beaten gold on his back and thick silver chains girding him like belts. Round his neck were more silver chains. They told me that on feast days he wore gold chains but silver chains when he was going to his bath."

Even more alluring stories resulted from Captain Cook's epic voyage to the South Pacific towards the end of the eighteenth century. The job of writing the official history was entrusted to a London literary figure named Dr. John Hawkesworth, who worked partly from Cook's journals, partly from interviews with the crew, and partly, perhaps, from his own imagination. What he produced was an idyllic picture of a tropical paradise, sun-struck isles where the girls were lush, lovely, and ever willing, and life was one long guilt-free party.

Faulty though it was in many details—it overlooked such distressing customs as infanticide and human sacrifice, plus the fact that some of the islanders were cannibals—this haunting image has proved remarkably durable. In *Typee*, based on his own experiences in the Marquesas, Herman Melville wrote wistfully of "lovely houris—groves of coconuts—coral reefs—tattooed chiefs—and bamboo temples, sunny valleys planted with breadfruit trees—carved canoes dancing on the flashing blue water". The natives, in his eyes, were "voluptuous," as well as "bountifully provided with all the sources of pure and natural enjoyment". The only thing wrong as far as he could see was the evil wrought by outsiders (particularly the missionaries) who were trying to destroy this paradise by forcing an alien culture upon it.

The usually sardonic Mark Twain found the Hawaiian islands, "tranquil as dawn in the Garden of Eden . . . the balmy fragrance of jasmine, oleander, and the Pride of India . . . dusky native women swooping by, free as the wind on fleet horses". And the romantic novelist Robert Louis Stevenson discovered his final home among the breathtaking beauties of Samoa, where, later, Margaret Mead did a pioneering study that seemed to show it was all actually true. (*Coming of Age in Samoa* became a surprise best-seller, probably the most widely read anthropological study ever written. A recently published book takes a dim view of Mead's findings, suggesting that many of them were based on wish-fulfilment; if so, she was thoroughly within the tradition of South Seas visitors.)

Paul Gauguin captured the bold colours of Tahiti on canvas and rhapsodized over its women: "These nymphs, I want to perpetuate them; with their golden skin, their searching animal odour, their tropical savours." Several years after Gauguin's death, Somerset Maugham turned up to research his novel *The Moon and Sixpence*, based on Gauguin's life, and found the same easy-going charm that had so bewitched Captain Cook's crew. His hero, thoroughly immoral by Western standards, is made to feel at home by the friendly islanders in their lava-lavas and fragrant frangipani leis: "In England and France he was the square peg in the round hole, but here the holes were any sort of shape and no sort of peg was quite round."

Nor is the lure any less effective today. The success of James Michener's *Tales of the South Pacific* was in large part based on it, and possibly the most memorable song in the Rodgers and Hammerstein musical was the haunting "Bali Hai," anthem to a tropical Shangri-La.

By that time, the real Bali was already firmly established as an earthly paradise. Shortly before the first world war a German doctor named Gregor Krause took a collection of haunting photographs, mostly of bare-breasted maidens in luxuriant tropical settings, that drew a talented collection of writers, painters, and dance enthusiasts to the island. These included Vicki Baum (author of *Grand Hotel*), who wrote a novel about it; Miguel Covarrubias, who settled down for a time and published a book of paintings still regarded as a classic; and such celebrities as Noel Coward and Charlie Chaplin. Coward was asked to record his impressions in the Bali Hotel's guest book, and contributed a tongue-in-cheek response to Bali's omnipresent artistic activity that went in part: "As I said this morning to Charlie/There is far too much music in Bali/And though as a place it's entrancing/There is also a thought too much dancing."

Joseph Conrad, from the moment he encountered it as a young man sailing through the Malay Archipelago, was enchanted by the East and filled his novels and stories with loving descriptions drawn from memories of Bangkok and the wild shores of Borneo. He was also one of the first to see the literary possibilities of the odd, sometimes larger-than-life characters who found their way to these strange places: his memorable Lord Jim is modelled on the equally extraordinary James Brooke, who carved a private empire out of the jungles of Sarawak and ruled it as the White Rajah.

For most Victorian readers, India was created largely by the gifted pen of Rudyard Kipling. Gunga Din and Kim and Mowgli were the companions of childhood, as were the marvellous non-human denizens of its colourful landscape. Kipling's romantic power was compelling even when he wrote about a place he had never seen and his facts were slightly awry, as in the case of "Mandalay". No flying fishes play on the "road" (i.e. the Irrawaddy River) that leads to the old Burmese capital, nor does the dawn come up "like thunder outer China 'crost the Bay"; but never mind, the tone of pure romance is exactly right:

> Ship me somewhere east of Suez, where the best is like the worst,
> Where there ain't no Ten Commandments an' a man can raise a thirst,
> For the temple bells are callin', and it's there that I would be
> By the old Moulmein Pagoda, looking lazy at the sea . . .

Wisely conceding India to Kipling, Maugham staked out British Malaya as his particular territory, concentrating on the aberrations of its rulers. Some of his plots—the murderous memsahibs, the interracial liaisons, the invariable twist of irony at the end—may seem slightly dated today, like the Edwardian comedies he wrote for the stage. But not the settings, not the atmosphere: the shadowy bungalows with the rattan furniture, tiffin on the verandah, *stengahs* at sundown, mosquito nets pale in the moonlight, the sinister stillness of a rubber plantation, bare brown feet padding across polished teak floors. Those were rendered with such lapidary precision they came to constitute an immensely real world of their own, still eagerly sought after by nostalgic travellers in such Maughamesque places as Singapore's Raffles Hotel.

Japan's image as a quaint land of cherry blossoms, doll-like geishas, and exquisitely contrived gardens began to take shape soon after Commander Matthew Perry arrived with his four black ships to end its long seclusion. Townsend Harris, the first American consul-general, contributed to it when he published the journals of his experience; but it found perhaps its most romantic expression in the works of Lafcadio Hearn.

Hearn became a Japanophile almost at once, as suggested in a sketch he wrote entitled "My First Day in the Orient", part of which reads as follows: "The street vistas, as seen above the dancing white mushroom-shaped hat of my sandaled runner, have an allurement of which I fancy I would never weary. Elfish everything seems; for everything as well as everybody is small, and queer, and mysterious; the little houses under their blue roofs, the little shop fronts hung with blue, and the smiling little people in their blue costumes . . . . And perhaps the supremely pleasurable impression of this morning is that produced by the singular gentleness of popular scrutiny. Everybody looks at you curiously, but there is never anything disagreeable, much less hostile in the gaze: most commonly it is accompanied by a smile or half-smile. And the ultimate consequence of all the curious kindly looks and smiles is that the stranger finds himself thinking of fairyland."

The smitten writer continued his love affair through numerous other articles and books, reaching a climax of sorts when he confessed, "I only wish I could be reincarnated in some little Japanese baby, so that I could feel the world as beautifully as a Japanese brain does."

Though few could equal the ardour of his expression, Hearn was only one of many Western writers who succumbed to Japan's charms. Even the war proved only a temporary dampener; within a few years the flame of romance was burning as brightly as ever in Michener's novel *Sayonara* and then in such evocations of the past as the best-selling *Shogun*.

Realists may complain, with some justice, that all these visions of the Orient have misled the vast public who responded so eagerly to them. Millions were starving in India while Halliburton was mooning in the pool at the Taj Mahal. Was Maugham unaware of the economics of the Malayan rubber industry? Japan may have seemed like a fairyland to Lafcadio Hearn, but it was also well on its way to becoming a formidable military power.

To which perhaps the only real answer is that the world needed romance—and still does for that matter, perhaps more than ever.

4

MURDER ON THE VERANDAH

On a hot, humid Sunday night in April 1911, a rickshaw driver waiting outside a bungalow in Kuala Lumpur was startled to hear two shots—a rare and frightening sound in that tranquil outpost of empire. Immediately afterwards he saw the Englishman he had brought to the place stagger down the steps from the verandah. Behind him came a European woman; she had a revolver in her hand and she kept firing it, again and again, until the man crumpled in the drive, some distance from the bungalow.

No one will ever know for sure what was going on in the mind of twenty-three-year-old Ethel Proudlock as she stood there in the tropical gloom, an empty gun in her hand and a dying man at her feet. Whatever her wildest imaginings, though, one can safely assume she was spared a glimpse into the future that would have horrified her as much as the murder she had just committed—the prospect of old-movie buffs watching her, nearly a century later, stalk across that verandah, thinly disguised as Bette Davis, firing those fatal shots with implacable fury.

The movie was *The Letter*, a classic based on Somerset Maugham's short story of the same title and the successful play he adapted from it. First published in his collection *The Casuarina Tree* in 1926, *The Letter* proved perhaps the most popular of all Maugham's tales of Englishmen living in remote places and has been anthologized countless times. It had everything his admirers expected: an exotic setting, seething passions that shattered the thin veneer of British gentility, and a masterly plot that built relentlessly to a climax both surprising and ironic. It was equally successful on the stage, in London with Gladys Cooper and on Broadway with Jeanne Eagles, and had been filmed once before the Davis version.

But in the Federated Malay States, and particularly in Kuala Lumpur, reactions were rather less enthusiastic. Even if readers there did not know that on one visit Maugham had stayed with E.A.S. Wagner, one of Ethel Proudlock's counsels, they were in no doubt at all as to the basis of the story. And while some of the more sensational details were drawn from gossip they themselves had spread and believed to be true, they were frankly furious to see it all in cold print. "If he had returned to Malaya," according to Maugham's biographer, Ted Morgan, "it is no exaggeration to say that he might have come to harm."

Though among readers he became as closely identified with Malaya as Kipling with India, Maugham in fact spent relatively little time there—a few months in 1921–22 and four months in 1925. After *The Letter* he prudently stayed away until 1959, near the end of his life, by which time Ethel Proudlock was forgotten, along with the society that had produced her and her case.

On the two earlier trips he travelled with a young American named Gerald Haxton. By almost all accounts, even friendly ones, Haxton was a thorough mess. He gambled, drank, and seduced young boys; he had been deported from England as an undesirable alien and forbidden ever to return. But he was the great love of Maugham's life and also, perhaps not incidentally, an invaluable asset to him as a writer.

Maugham was afflicted with a painful stammer and was naturally shy of strangers. Haxton, on the other hand, as Maugham later wrote in an appreciation, "had an amiability of disposition that enabled him in a very short time to make friends with people in ships, clubs, barrooms, and hotels, so that through him I was able to get into easy contact with an immense number of persons whom otherwise I should have known only from a distance."

In their travels they met a number of outstanding "characters", larger-than-life figures who seemed to have stepped from the pages of a novel or short shory. They also met dozens of bored planters and district officers and their wives, who doubtless were delighted to find two strangers not only unfamiliar with local gossip but gratifyingly eager to hear it repeated over a congenial drink. Even those aware of Maugham's literary renown were lulled into indiscretions by his polite reticence and by Haxton's boozy good nature.

Many of them paid a price for their casual revelations. On one occasion some acquaintances in Singapore invited them to meet a couple who were in the city on a holiday from the jungle of North Borneo. The husband of the couple was a British civil official, and before they arrived Maugham's hostess could not resist imparting some juicy background titbits. It seemed that the official had once been a confirmed drunkard who went to bed with a bottle every night. "He became so tiresome," Maugham recorded in his notebook, "that the Governor sent him home on leave and told him that if he didn't sober up he would have to dismiss him. The man was a bachelor, and the Governor advised him to find a nice girl in England and marry her, and she would keep him straight. At the end of his leave, he came back married and a reformed character."

When the subjects of the conversation arrived, they turned out to be an ordinary, rather dull couple. But Maugham's literary imagination was sparked by the slight oddity of their past. "I never saw them again," he later wrote in a footnote to his notebook entry, "and they never knew what they had let themselves in for when they came to dinner that night. They suggested to me a story which I called *Before the Party*."

It seems unlikely, however, that the poor couple never knew. Their Singapore hostess must certainly have read *Before the Party* when it appeared a few years later, and it is hard to believe she refrained from spreading the news of what her distinguished visitor had done with the amusing little predinner tale. He had, in fact, used it almost exactly as it had been told, up to a point. But then he had the husband return to his bottle after a time, whereupon his wife cuts his throat with a razor-sharp *parang* and passes it off as suicide.

In *The Letter*, the distinction between truth and fiction was so slight as to be almost non-existent. Maugham made a number of changes, both major and minor—not to spare the feelings of anybody involved but to give the story a better dramatic shape. The locale of the bungalow, for instance, was shifted from a rather mundane Kuala Lumpur suburb to a lonely rubber estate; the husband became a hearty planter instead of acting headmaster of a school; and some ten years were added to the heroine's age.

The physical description of Leslie Crosbie, however, could well have been applied to Ethel Proudlock: "a fragile creature, neither short nor tall, and graceful rather than pretty." And her lawyer's opinion was certainly what Maugham must have heard many times in 1922: "She was the last woman in the world to commit murder."

Yet she had, and the tantalizing question was why. Ethel Proudlock's explanation was almost exactly the same as that given by calm, collected Mrs. Crosbie, and she never changed it once during the long hours of questioning.

The former manager of a tin mine in Salak South, a few miles outside Kuala Lumpur, William Steward (called Hammond in the story) had been a casual friend of the Proudlocks for several years, she said. One or two times he had come to them to listen to music but always by appointment and only when William Proudlock was present. She was therefore surprised to find him at her door on the evening in question, when her husband was out for dinner with a friend. After a perfectly innocent conversation (about religion, said Mrs. Proudlock), he surprised her far more by suddenly putting his arms around her and saying he loved her.

She asked him if he was mad. ("Don't be an idiot. Sit down where you were before and talk sensible or else I shall send you home," is the way Maugham's Mrs. Crosbie expresses it.) Instead of replying he held her tightly and began to lift her skirt. In the frantic struggle that ensued her hand "came into contact with a revolver," one she kept handy when her husband was away. She remembered firing the first two shots but not the others. When she came to her senses, the gun was empty and Steward was lying in the drive.

Public opinion strongly supported Mrs. Proudlock. Though probably Eurasian (a point unmentioned by Maugham), she was a highly respectable woman, a diligent singer every Sunday in the choir of St. Mary's Church (now the Anglican Cathedral). Besides being a teacher, her husband was a member of the local football team and president of the Selangor State Band. When it was learned that Steward had been living with a Chinese woman—an unforgiveable sin in the eyes of the European ladies of the community—her plight aroused even more sympathy, for such a man was clearly capable of attempted rape.

Cooler heads, though, were disturbed by one aspect of the tragedy from the very beginning. "I should be wanting in my duty as your legal adviser," the lawyer tells Robert Crosbie early in the Maugham story, "If I did not tell you there is one point which causes me just a little anxiety. If your wife had only shot Hammond once, the whole thing would be absolutely plain sailing. Unfortunately, she fired six times." Later, to Leslie Crosbie, he puts it more bluntly: "It was hard to accept the possibility that a delicate, frightened, and habitually self-controlled woman, of gentle nature and refined instincts, should have surrendered to an absolutely, uncontrolled frenzy."

Officials in Kuala Lumpur wondered the same thing about Mrs.

Proudlock, and that was why she was committed for trial by a judge and two assessors on a charge of first degree murder.

It is at this point that the famous letter turns up in Maugham's story. Offered for sale through a Chinese clerk in the lawyer's office, its implications are devastating to Mrs. Crosbie's defence; for it proves not only that Hammond came at her request but also that the request was hardly that of a casual acquaintance ("I absolutely must see you . . . I am desperate and if you don't come I won't answer for the consequences . . .").

The damning document is finally bought from the dead man's Chinese mistress for $10,000, and without it the trial does indeed prove "plain sailing". Mrs. Crosbie is found innocent after only five minutes of deliberation, a decision that is greeted by "a great outburst of applause" from the crowded courtroom.

Only that is not the end of the story, of course. The big scene, the one both audience and actress have been waiting for, is still to come. Leslie Crosbie's calm exterior breaks apart, and, left alone with her lawyer, she spills out the horrifying truth. Hammond was her lover, she summoned him because of his affair with the Chinese woman, and his confession sent her into a mad rage: "And then I don't know what happened. I was beside myself. I saw red. I seized the revolver and I fired. He gave a cry and I saw I'd hit him. He staggered and rushed for the verandah. I ran after him and fired again. He fell and then I stood over him and I fired and fired until the revolver went click, click and I knew there were no more cartridges."

After this extraordinary outburst ("Her face was no longer human, it was distorted with cruelty, and rage and pain . . ."), she composes herself, becomes once more "the wellbred and even distinguished woman". When the lawyer's wife calls, she answers "I'm coming, Dorothy dear. I'm sorry to give you so much trouble." And so the story ends.

In real life there was no letter; nor was there any confessional outburst, at least as far as anyone knows. But the climax was, if anything, even more shocking than Maugham's imaginative embroidery.

Ethel Proudlock stuck resolutely to her story. She said she had met Steward at the Selangor Club on the day before the crime and suggested that he drop by some time to see her and her husband. But she denied inviting him the following evening when she knew her husband would be out. She also denied that she had gone to Salak South to see Steward while William Proudlock was abroad in 1909 and 1910.

A search of Steward's house revealed no communication from her, no proof of any intimate relationship. Two people testified Steward told them he had an appointment Sunday night, but they did not know where.

The only real weakness in Mrs. Proudlock's story was the number of shots fired. Like Leslie Crosbie, she claimed she could not remember the final four. Another point that caused some raised eyebrows was the fact that she had nothing on under the rather elaborate gown in which she was supposedly spending a quiet evening at home alone; she explained this by telling the court, "It is not my habit to wear drawers when I wear a frock with thick lining."

To most of her supporters—who then included the majority of the British community—Ethel Proudlock's acquittal seemed a foregone conclusion. They were thus staggered when her judges found her guilty and sentenced her to death by hanging.

The next few weeks saw a frenzy of activity on behalf of the condemned woman. The newspapers were filled with angry letters protesting the verdict. William Proudlock sent a telegram to King George asking for a pardon, and sixty European women sent a similar one to Queen Mary. Some two hundred Europeans signed another petition, and in Penang $2,000 was raised to finance the appeal she had filed. Emotions even crossed the rigid racial lines of colonial society: 560 Indian residents petitioned for her release.

In the middle of all this, a little-known fact came to light. Due to the complex system of alliances by which the British controlled Malaya, the only person with the power to pardon Mrs. Proudlock was the Sultan of Selangor, acting on the "advice" of the British Resident. If she lost her appeal, he was the one who would decide her fate.

Ethel Proudlock then took a step that surprised many of those convinced of her innocence. She suddenly withdrew her appeal and threw herself on the mercy of the Sultan. Why? She never explained, but now disquieting rumours began to circulate, undoubtedly the same ones Maugham heard a decade later. She was afraid, it was whispered, that a new trial would unearth evidence to show that she had gone to see Steward at Salak South; they were more than casual friends; in that overstaffed world, servants were omnipresent, perhaps one of them had noticed something.

Whatever her motives, they resulted in her freedom. In July 1911, without objection from the Resident, the Sultan granted her a free pardon. Two days later she left for Penang, where she took the next ship to England.

William Proudlock stayed behind for a time. He, too, eventually found himself in a courtroom when he accused a policeman of having beaten two of his servants in an effort to get information about the case from them. The policeman denied the accusation, countersued for libel, and won. His reputation now seriously damaged, Proudlock resigned from the school and followed his wife.

Only sketchy details are known about the subsequent fortunes of the Proudlocks. They emigrated to Canada and later Ethel, without her husband, entered the United States and ended up in Florida. Reports that she died in an insane asylum appear to be unfounded. Considering the widespread success of *The Letter* on stage it is thus quite possible that, like the couple from Borneo, she knew all too well what Maugham had done with her sad story.

5

ISLE OF SERENDIPITOUS SPLENDOURS

arly Arab traders who braved the perils of the Indian Ocean in search of rare gems and even rarer spices called Sri Lanka Serendip, "the isle of delights". The name so appealed to the English essayist Horace Walpole that in 1754 he was inspired to write a fairy story entitled *The Three Princes of Serendip*, in which the heroes, looking for one thing, were constantly finding something else even more delightful. To describe this pleasant phenomenon, Walpole coined the useful word "serendipity", meaning the "faculty of making happy and unexpected discoveries".

The experiences of a long line of sensitive travellers to the island have indeed been serendipitous if the extraordinary number of literary observations it has inspired are to be believed. I had been struck in my reading about the place by the near unanimity of enthusiasm, not only from obscure scribblers but also some of the leading lights of English and American letters. It was to search out the sources of this enchantment that I went to what the Sinhalese themselves call the "Resplendent Isle". (The name Ceylon, which the British adapted from the Portuguese Ceilao, was discarded in 1972.)

The first known Englishman to describe Sri Lanka was a young sailor with the East India Company named Ronald Knox, and he was not only captivated but captured, with literary results that still reverberate.

Knox happened to come ashore in 1660 when the island was being ruled by Rajasingha II, the king of the central city of Kandy. Some kings collect jewels, others beautiful women; Rajasingha, it seems, collected Europeans. Over the years he built up quite a menagerie of them, numbering some 500 by the end of his reign. They were well treated, comfortably quartered both in Kandy and in several outlying villages, whose inhabitants were under strict royal instructions to keep them supplied with all they wanted short of freedom.

Ronald Knox spent nineteen years in these odd circumstances. Though he never gave up his dream of going home, as many of his fellow captives did (without much grief one gathers), he settled down and even went into business as a trader. He eventually succeeded in making his way to one of the Dutch-held towns on the coast and, in 1680, returned to an England that had almost forgotten him.

An Historical Relation of Ceylon, the account he wrote of his experiences, created a sensation. Two English editions appeared, and it was translated into Dutch, German, and French during his lifetime, making Knox one of the celebrities of his day. Among its most enthusiastic readers was Daniel Defoe, who was born in the same year Knox was captured and who was just starting his literary career. Defoe never forgot the resourceful sailor who made the best of a difficult situation. When he wrote *Robinson Crusoe*, he borrowed the basic idea from the story of Alexander Selkirk, stranded for four-and-a-half years on the island of Juan Fernandez in the South Pacific, but he clearly modelled the pragmatic Crusoe on Knox's self-portrait.

While Knox was compelled by force to remain in Sri Lanka, most subsequent visitors lingered there by choice. In my own explorations I followed the lead of the majority of the writers I had read. I passed quickly through Colombo when I arrived and headed southward along a series of picture-postcard beaches of dazzling white sand, graceful coconut palms, and improbably brilliant turquoise water.

The beauty of Sri Lanka's coast increased the further south I went, one spectacular beach succeeding another until they became almost commonplace. Then, at the little fishing village of Weligama near the southern tip, I suddenly saw the island.

It rose only fifty yards or so offshore, accessible by foot during low tide—a rocky mound covered with a lush mini-jungle of tropical trees and shrubs through which could be glimpsed a magical house that seemed largely composed of windows and terraces. It was a toy island almost, the sort of fantasy place conjured up in South-Sea-island dreams. Though I had seen it only once before in a blurred black-and-white photograph, I knew instantly that it was Taprobane, a place that had long stirred literary imaginations.

The little island owes its name and much of its charm to a European aristocrat named the Comte de Mauny-Talvande, who first came to Sri Lanka in 1911 as a guest of Sir Thomas Lipton, the tea magnate. The count fell in love with the languid, tropical atmosphere and embarked on a search for "one spot which, by its sublime beauty, would fulfil my dreams and hold me there for life". It took a long time, more than ten years, for Sri Lanka was frustratingly full of such spots: "There were times when I told myself I have found it, but a few steps further on it was still more beautiful." Finally, his "endless, seeking destiny" brought him to Weligama, and there at last he beheld his "Isle of Dreams".

Swimming across the narrow stretch of water, he climbed to the highest point. "I sat for a long time on a boulder overhanging the sea," he later wrote, "wishing that this island lost in the Indian Ocean were mine; picturing and planning what I should do with it. I felt my heart beating with the overwhelming desire to create, the pride of creation, and to find in it peace, the nearest thing to happiness. Yes, it would, it must, be the home which I had dreamed of so many years past."

And so it became. He changed the name from Galduwa, Sinhalese for "rocky island", to Taprobane, the old Greek name for Sri Lanka, and then proceeded to build on it an extraordinary octagonal house. His plan, according to a later resident, was not for "a real house with an interior", but for "a pavilion which would be a continuation of the landscape outside, and from every part of which there would be multiple views. And so, blithely, he did away with walls between the rooms so that all nine rooms (including the bathrooms) would in reality be only one, and that one open to the wind . . . . The result is very rational and, like most things born of fanaticism, wildly impractical."

Wildly impractical or not, Taprobane suited the count's romantic temperament perfectly, and he lived there in contentment for 18 years, until age and World War II forced him to part with it. The little island was also to suit the author of the description just quoted, the American writer Paul Bowles, another restless artist looking for an exotic home. ("Two types of landscape have always had the power to stimulate me, the desert and the tropical forest. These two extremes of natural terrain—one with the minimum and the other with the greatest possible amount of vegetation—are both capable of sending me into a state bordering on euphoria.") He bought the house in 1950 and enjoyed his paradise for an annual stay of six months until 1956, when personal reasons obliged him to give it up.

(One of the reasons may have been the attitude of his wife Jane, also a noted writer. "When I broke the news of the purchase to [her], her reaction was less enthusiastic than I might have desired. 'I think you're crazy!' she cried. 'An island off the coast of Ceylon? How do you get there?' I explained that you took a ship through the Mediterranean and the Red Sea, crossed part of the Indian Ocean, landed at Colombo, and hopped on a train which let you off at the fishing village of Weligama. 'And once you're on the island there's nothing between you and the South Pole,' I added. She looked at me for a long moment. 'You'll never get me there,' she said.")

Bowles was not the last writer to fall under the spell of Taprobane. Robin Maugham, Somerset's novelist nephew, seriously considered buying it in the early 1970s when he, too, was looking for "a place of contentment". He backed out at the last minute, partly because he felt a new highway on the mainland had compromised the island's blissful sense of isolation, mostly because of his own shortcomings. Faced with a choice between "the benefits of civilization on the one hand and the glories of unimpaired nature on the other," he wrote in *Search for Nirvana*, he had no doubt that one should opt for the latter. "But for most people, alas," he concluded, "this requires a particular cast of character and many years of training. I have an uneasy feeling that I personally have begun too late."

I could have lived with the highway. Standing on it, looking across at Taprobane, I was trying to decide what time the tide went out when the driver honked and called on me to hurry if I wanted to reach Hambantota by sundown.

Hambantota offered the last views of the sea before heading inland for the hill country. It also has literary associations, for it was here that the young Leonard Woolf passed some of his happiest days and also came to some momentous decisions concerning his future life.

Woolf arrived on the island toward the end of 1904 to begin what he thought was a career in the Ceylon Civil Service. "I was going to a place and life in which I really had not the faintest idea of how I should live and what I should be doing," he wrote sixty five years later. "All that I was taking with me from the old life as a contribution to the new and to prepare me for my task of helping to rule the British Empire was ninety large beautifully printed volumes of Voltaire and a wire-haired fox terrier."

Though forced to erect a facade to hide his intelligence ("the social defect I have suffered from ever since I was a child") when associating with hearty tea planters and unimaginative officials—he does not say how he hid those ninety volumes of Voltaire—Woolf proved an able administrator. Over a tour of seven years he held increasingly important posts, first in the northern district of Jaffna, then in Kandy, finally in Hambantota. And he loved the island, especially Hambantota, then a remote jungled district teeming with wildlife, where his work often cut him off from other Europeans for weeks at a time.

But toward the end of his stay, he came more and more to feel that he was "playing a part in an exciting play on a brightly coloured stage" or "living a story by Kipling". More basically, as George Orwell was to do later in Burma, he began to have doubts about the empire, certainly about his role in it. When he returned to England on leave in 1911, the lure of Ceylon was still powerful enough for him to entertain vague fantasies of settling down in Hambantota with a Sinhalese wife; but the bracing intellectual air of Bloomsbury, and particularly a renewed relationship with the strange, talented Virginia Stephen, soon dispelled such dreams. On the eve of his scheduled return, he resigned from the service and went on to his true destiny as Virginia's husband, though also as the author of a nostalgic novel called *The Village in the Jungle* about life in far-off Hambantota.

Sri Lanka has been described as a universe in miniature with a variety of culture, scenery, and climate rare in even much larger countries. One perceives the truth of this as one ascends into the cool hill country, where English roses and rhododendrons flourish beside towering tree ferns and Victorian-style hotels have fireplaces in the lounge. Around Kandy innumerable spice gardens line the road, the owners of which are all eager to inform the ignorant tourist that cinnamon is actually a bark, that vanilla is the seed of a climbing orchid, and that nutmeg and mace are part of the same fruit.

Spices were a significant part of Sri Lanka's legendary appeal, and few of its literary visitors were able to resist quoting the famous lines:

What though the spicy breezes
Blow soft o'er Ceylon's isle . . .

Most of them, indeed, not only quoted but insisted that the breezes actually *were* spicy, sometimes from quite a distance. "A fragrance of cinnamon and cloves with a base of coconut oil reaches our noses before our eyes can detect the waving tufts of palms on the horizon," wrote Achsah Barlow Brewster, a wealthy artist who with her husband Earl later settled in a rambling bungalow overlooking Kandy where they had D.H. Lawrence as a visitor in 1922. (He complained of the heat, and repaid the Brewster's hospitality by satirizing them in a short story.) Such a literal interpretation, however, was firmly scotched by an earlier visitor, a U.S. Navy surgeon named William S.W. Ruschenberger. In *A Voyage Round the World*, he calls the celebrated description "a pious imposition palmed upon us by an idle race of people, called poets . . . . Such breezes never swept the olfactories of any man, unless they were wafted from some grocer's shop or cook's pantry."

The pious poet who wrote the lines was Bishop Reginald Heber of the Society for the Propagation of the Gospel. They were part of "From Greenland's Icy Mountains", composed in 1811 and perhaps the most famous missionary hymn of all time. Its stirring strains inspired countless evangelists to set sail for remote shores all over the world, including those of Sri Lanka, undeterred by the ominous warning that followed the promise of sensory pleasures:

Where every prospect pleases
And only man is vile;
In vain with lavish kindness
The gifts of God are strewn;

The heathen in his blindness
Bows down to wood and stone.

Many of the writers who came to the island were quick to dispute the Bishop's opinion of the inhabitants. "Man is not vile in this beautiful island, but gentle and patient and good," insisted Margaret Mordecai, an American traveller, in a book called *Indian Dreamlands*. And Mark Twain, who visited in 1876 on a round-the-world tour, expressed disapproval of the missionary influence on local attire. After an admiring look at what he called the "Oriental conflagrations of costume"—"such stunning colours, such intensely vivid colours, such rich and exquisite minglings and fusions of rainbows and lightnings! And all harmonious"—he cast a beady eye at the dress of a group of Sinhalese girls marching out of a Christian school: "Ugly, barbarous, destitute of taste, destitute of grace, repulsive as a shroud. I looked at my women folk's clothes—just full-grown duplicates of the outrages disguising these poor little abused creatures—and was ashamed to be seen in the streets with them. Then I looked at my own clothes and was ashamed to be seen in the street with myself."

But some of the missionaries found time to respond to Sri Lanka's lush charms even while busily strewing the gifts of God. "I think it must be the most beautiful place in the world," Phillips Brooks, Rector of Boston's Trinity Church (and, incidentally, the first American invited to preach at Westminster Abbey), was moved to write a relative soon after his arrival in Kandy in 1883. The noted divine was further inspired to compose a whimsical verse that began:

> Oh, this beautiful island of Ceylon!
> With the cocoanut-trees on the shore;
> It is shaped like a pear with the peel on
> And Kandy lies at the core.

and ended, a bit desperately:

The tongue they speak mostly is Tamil
Which sounds you can hardly tell how
It is half like the scream of a camel,
And half like the grunt of a sow.

Other writers have been profoundly moved by the spiritual quality
of Sri Lanka's Buddhist monuments. One was Thomas Merton, the
former Trappist monk and author of *The Seven-Storey Mountain*, who
came toward the end of 1968 on an Asian pilgrimage to explore the
relations between Christian and Buddhist mysticism. The fabled
beaches and jungles held no allure for him; not until he reached
Kandy (where he preached a sermon in the Cathedral) did he begin
to feel anything, and not until he went to the ancient city of
Polonnaruwa the next day did he have a remarkable revelation.

Unlike Anuradhapura, Sri Lanka's other great Buddhist site,
where pilgrims flock to the numerous shrines and partake in colourful ceremonies around a bodhi tree alleged to be more than 2,000
years old, Polonnaruwa is pervaded by a strange stillness. This is particularly true of a place called Gal Vihara. According to Merton's
journal: "The path dips down to Gal Vihara; a wide, quiet, hollow,
surrounded with trees. A low outcrop of rock, with a cave cut into it,
a reclining Buddha on the right, and Ananda, I guess, standing by the
head of the reclining Buddha. In the cave, another seated Buddha . . .
Looking at these figures I was suddenly, almost forcibly, jerked clean
out of the habitual, half-tied vision of things, and an inner clearness,
clarity, as if exploding from the rocks themselves, became evident and
obvious . . . I don't know when in my life I have ever had such a sense
of beauty and spiritual validity running together in one aesthetic illumination. Surely, with Mahabalipuram and Polonnaruwa my Asian
pilgrimage has come clear and purified itself. I mean, I know and have
seen what I was obscurely looking for. I don't know what else remains

but I have now seen and pierced through the surface and have got beyond the shadow and the disguise. This is Asia in its purity, not covered over with garbage, Asian or European or American, and it is clear, pure complete. It says everything; it needs nothing. And because it needs nothing it can afford to be silent, unnoticed, undiscovered. It does not need to be discovered. It is we, Asians included, who need to discover it."

His discovery was tragically well-timed. Only a week later, while trying to plug in a faulty fan in a Bangkok guest house, he was electrocuted. His lifetime search for "the home where I have never been in this body" was over—had already ended, perhaps in the profound silence of Gal Vihara.

A Hollywood spectacular, with some young Laurence Olivier gorgeously costumed in one of Twain's "conflagrations' could well be based on the saga of Sigiriya. This sheer 500-foot monolith of granite, which rises dramatically out of the dry central plain, boasts a dark history of almost Shakespearean dimensions. Here, in the fifth century, a ruler named Kassapa usurped the throne from his father and then had him buried alive in an embankment. Fearful of a half-brother who had sworn revenge, Kassapa retreated to Sigiriya, where he built a lavish palace on the broad, flat summit, accessible only by a narrow path cut into the rock. Here he ruled for eighteen nervous years, surrounding himself with objects of beauty (including some fine frescoes of bare-breasted women that still glow from the walls of a gallery halfway up) but always watching the horizon for the approach of his Nemesis.

It finally came, with results that would have gratified any Greek playwright. In the confusion of battle, Kassapa's men mistakenly thought he was retreating and deserted him, whereupon he slashed his own throat and died in the shadow of his impregnable fortress.

With such rich material one might expect any number of philosophical meditations or fat historical novels inspired by Sigiriya; but tragedy, perhaps, strikes a jarring note in Sri Lanka's lush landscape. Only one of the writers I read seems to have been stirred by the place, and then not by its history but by its physical oddity. To science fiction writer Arthur C. Clarke the huge, flat-topped mass of rock suggested a mysterious platform. With his futuristic imagination, he had no difficulty in carrying the idea a few steps further and, in one of his novels, using the rock as the base of a space elevator that transports passengers up into the stars.

The object of a considerable cult ever since *2001: A Space Odyssey*, written in collaboration with Stanley Kubrick, Clarke is certainly Sri Lanka's leading literary resident today. I read *The View from Serendip*, his collection of partly autobiographical essays, in assorted places around the island—lolling on a beach up the coast from Taprobane, snuggling under a comforter in the chilly hill station of Nuwara Eliya, sitting on the verandah of a guest house with a view of brooding Sigiriya.

Describing "the process of being Serendipidized", which began for him in the 1950s, he tends to be brisk and down-to-earth rather than eloquent and mystical. Only rarely does he allow emotion to show, as when writing of the "exquisite arc of beach" that sealed his determination to stay forever. Throughout, though, one recognizes the voice of the true romantic, the same voice I had heard in so many of the island's admirers, from the equally no-nonsense Ronald Knox to the troubled Thomas Merton.

Few of them shared Clarke's luck in being able to glimpse their Eden and have it too. But all of them, I think, would have responded to what he calls "the most beautiful tribute ever paid" to the Resplendent Isle, offered some six hundred years ago by a papal legate: "From Ceylon to Paradise, according to native tradition, is forty miles; there may be heard the sounds of the fountains of Paradise."

6

GHOSTS ALONG THE CHAO PHRAYA RIVER

I grew up in a small Georgia town on the banks of a river identified on maps as the Flint. It was never known as the Flint to me, however. I preferred the infinitely more poetic Thronateeska, which was what the original inhabitants of the region had called it, and on childhood rambles I delighted in populating the muddy, rather mundane stream with armadas of war canoes, filled with fierce befeathered braves ready to do bloody battle against the dull white men who had founded the town I knew.

This tendency to invest present sites with the trappings of a more colourful past has persisted, especially in riverine surroundings. It returned with particular potency when I came to live in Bangkok and began to explore the great Chao Phraya River, which was then still one of the city's major means of communication and was also, as I discovered, rich in ghosts of the most evocative kind.

Unlike most visitors, even in those days, I arrived in Thailand by river, aboard a Dutch freighter that had brought me all the way from New York—a journey that took all of eight weeks and cost the princely sum of $500 for a private stateroom and four meals a day. I passed a lot of time on the voyage reading up on my future home, so I already had a few river ghosts to start my collection when we crossed the bar at Pak Nam ("river mouth") and began the final approach to the capital.

Waiting there at Pak Nam, for instance, I found the dignified shade of Sir John Bowring, Governor of Hong Kong, Minister Plenipotentiary to China, and accredited to the courts of Japan,

Korea, Siam, and Vietnam. A man of perception and great diplomatic skill, he had been invited by the ruler of Siam, the re-doubtable King Mongkut, and he would later describe that 1855 visit as "one of the most interesting parts of my public life". Though it lasted barely a month, it resulted in a warm friendship between Bowring and the King, and, more important for Thailand's future, a pioneering trade treaty that led to revolutionary changes in the country.

I knew all about Bowring from his two-volume study entitled *The Kingdom and the People of Siam*, and it took only a slight exercise of the imagination to find him sailing up the Chao Phraya beside me, though in considerably grander style. The King had sent quite a reception committee to greet the envoy, together with a selection of native fruits—one of which, Bowring notes, was "salutory in cases of dysentery", surely a thoughtful gift for any newcomer.

The welcomers also brought eight state barges and six smaller craft to escort the visitors to the capital. "Mine was magnificent," Bowring wrote approvingly. "It had the gilded and emblazoned image of an idol at its prow, with two flags like vanes grandly ornamented. Near the stern was a carpeted divan, with scarlet and gold curtains. The boat was also richly gilded and had a tail like a fish. The captain stood at the head; but the boat was steered by two persons with oars, who constantly excited the rowers to exert themselves, and called up the spirit of the most active competition."

In the mist of my first early morning on the Chao Phraya I imagined this splendid creation making its glittering way upstream, taking Bowring on his momentous mission a century before. Hardly had it vanished around a bend in the river than I was joined by another ghost from a slightly later date, this one a prim but somehow exotic looking English lady in Victorian dress, with a pair of non-Thai servants and a small child. She had an apprehensive expression, as well she might since she was in the process of obliterating a rather unsavoury past (poverty, mixed blood, a lowly husband recently dead) and was coming to teach English to some of King Mongkut's children.

She was, of course, none other than Mrs. Anna Leonowens, probably not the first person to reinvent herself in Bangkok and certainly not the last. (I have known at least two of ordinary birth who transformed themselves into titled dignitaries, and one who transformed himself into a middle-aged woman.) She was so successful at the effort that even her children never knew about her early days, and numerous actresses have obligingly portrayed her as the plucky gentlewoman she pretended to be, romping with her royal master in *The King and I.*

As we travelled together up the river, though, all this was in the future, and she was merely a worried woman en route to an unknown destiny. We parted company shortly after reaching Bangkok, where friends were waiting on the dock for me but where Anna was greeted with the discouraging news that no provision had been made for even putting her up on the first night.

"The situation was as Oriental as the scene," she later wrote in her famous memoirs, "heartless arbitrary insolence on the part of my employers; homelessness, forlornness, helplessness, mortification, indignation on mine . . . . My tears fell thick and fast and, weary and despairing, I closed my eyes, and tried to shut out heaven and earth; but the reflection would return to mock and goad me that, by my own act, I had placed myself in this position."

Poor Anna: she was a brave woman—"in fact", as Alexander Griswold has written, "a good deal braver than necessary if she could have seen how groundless her fears were"—and, as her freshly-minted past suggests, an imaginative one, too; but it is probably safe to say she could hardly have foreseen her eventual metamorphosis into the heroine of a Broadway musical comedy.

"I am located in the building called the English Factory," wrote

Bowring after his more auspicious landing, "but the building has been reconstructed, and put in good order for my reception. I occupy two apartments above—a sitting room, large and airy, and a bedroom, which has been newly papered, in which I sleep in a bed which is ornamented with drapery of cloth of scarlet and gold, and from which garlands of flowers are suspended."

It was only after I had lived in Bangkok for some years that I added the builder of this "factory" to my Chao Phraya ghosts. His name was Robert Hunter, and he was an English trader who arrived in the Thai capital around 1820—opium was among the more dubious commodities in which he dealt—and though his contributions to history are less celebrated than Bowring's, they were picturesque enough to make him irresistible to me.

Like almost every other non-royal resident of Bangkok in those early days (the city was not quite forty years old), Hunter lived at first on a houseboat anchored in the river a few miles down from the Grand Palace. Another English visitor of the time, E.A. Neale, says that it was "double the size of the others, very neatly painted, and well-furnished, with a nice little verandah in front".

These amenities apparently soon palled on Hunter. He became quite a prominent figure in Bangkok—the recognized leader, in fact, of the small foreign community—and perhaps he felt a more distinctive residence was in order. Or perhaps he viewed the houseboat as hazardous: Neale, on the very night of his arrival, attended a dinner party there "with all the English and Portuguese then assembled in Bangkok" and got so carried away with the festivities that he accidentally fell into the river and would have drowned had assistance not come.

In any event, Hunter used his royal connections to gain permission to build a proper house on the west bank of the river, not far from the present Memorial Bridge (the first, incidentally, to span the Chao Phraya, opened in 1932). It was the first Western-style private dwelling in Bangkok—a "very fine large prominent house, opposite to which the British ensign proudly floated on feast days and high days," according to Neale, who continued to enjoy Hunter's hospitality with less risk to life and limb.

Two decades later, Hunter was banished from the kingdom following a dispute with King Rama III in the course of which he rashly threatened to fire a cannon ball into the royal palace. His Thai-born wife and children remained at *hong huntraa*, as the combination house and trading company was known to Thais, and the eldest son, also named Robert, served as an official interpreter under King Mongkut, entertaining such foreign guests as Bowring. Robert Jr. joined the Chao Phraya ghosts in 1865 when, so recorded the American missionary Dr. Dan Beach Bradley, he went "on a drunken spree of many days' duration . . . fell off his dock and died of drowning, as so many do in Bangkok".

Besides his contribution to Bangkok architecture, Hunter is also remembered for something that happened late one afternoon in 1824, not long after he moved into his house. He was crossing the river on his way home when, according to Bradley, "his eye was caught by a strange object moving through the water at a considerable distance from his boat. It was a creature that appeared to have two heads, four arms, and four legs, all of which were moving in perfect harmony. As Mr. Hunter watched, the object climbed into a nearby boat, and to his amazement he realized that he had been looking at two small boys who were joined together at the chest".

These were the famous Siamese twins, Eng and Chang, appropriately referred to by present-day Thais as "Engchang". Then thirteen years old, they had but recently come to Bangkok from their birthplace near Pak Nam. Hunter became their friend and later, with an American sea captain named Abel Coffin, formed a partnership that sent the twins off to fame and fortune abroad. They never returned to

Thailand; eventually becoming American citizens, they married sisters and settled in North Carolina, producing a total of twelve children; but I never pass the site of *hong huntraa* without peering closely at the crowds of children who still swim in the Chao Phraya along the bank, hoping to spot an unusual synchronization of brown limbs.

Similarly, when I look across toward the Bangkok side at approximately the same place I always see another ghost, this one decidedly less appealing. Today the riverbank is lined with shophouses and the huge Pak Klong Market, an important centre for wholesale fruits, flowers, and vegetables, but for a time in the 1830s the area was left ominously empty. "Your boatmen shudder as you pass this place," wrote F.A. Neale, "and so do you when you learn the sad tale that has doomed that spot to perpetual solitude."

What happened was that the prince of a remote province rebelled against the king and, following his defeat, was brought to Bangkok for punishment. Death was decreed, of course, but of a special kind. First his eyes were put out with hot irons and then he was placed in a metal cage, "suspended just so high above the waters of the river that the unfortunate captive, by stretching his arms through the close iron bars, could barely manage to touch the ripple of the waters with the extreme tip of his fingers".

After three days and nights, the prince eventually died of thirst. By that time the floating houses in the neighborhood had already moved to a less harrowing location; they remained away until the memory faded among those whose fear of ghosts was less powerful than their appreciation of a choice piece of Chao Phraya real estate.

Other figures, too, return from the past to haunt me as I explore the waterway described by Henri Mouhot, the man who rediscovered the ruins of Angkor in 1860, as Bangkok's "high street and boulevard". Sometimes, for instance, as I pass the garden adjoining the Portuguese embassy (now part of the compound of the Royal Orchid

Sheraton Hotel), I espy a shadowy group sitting in the shade of a huge tamarind tree. One of them, I know, is Signor Marsinello de Rosa, Portuguese consul during Neale's time, and the others are American missionaries who once lived nearby.

Here, wrote Neale, the consul "had constructed a few pretty garden seats and reared a few choice flowers. And on this spot of a morning, before the sun's rays had waxed too warm, and of an evening after the heat of the day had passed, the consul and his sedate neighbours used to assemble and discuss the latest news of the day, or watch the gay scene the river presented, or turn to more gloomy themes and moralize on life and its many uncertain tenures".

One or twice I thought I glimpsed King Mongkut, Bowring's friend and Anna's master, on what must have been an extraordinary procession in 1851, involving no fewer than 269 magnificently carved barges, 50 accommodating boats, and 10,000 oarsmen chanting in the sunlight. (By contrast, a much-admired Royal Barge Procession in 1982, on the occasion of Bangkok's Bicentennial, boasted only 51 vessels.) This was the first year of his reign, and it may well have been the excursion that prompted him to issue an edict that reveals the true character of this remarkable man.

By tradition, when such processions took place, all the houses and buildings along the river were cleared of their residents and windows and doors securely closed. Wrote King Mongkut in his edict: "Such a practice is graciously considered by His Majesty to be more harmful than good. In the first place, those among the people who are acquainted with His Majesty are deprived of an opportunity to see him. In the second place, houses and shops with closed windows provide the best hiding places for those who wish to hide, among whom none can distinguish between sane men and lunatics. It is hereby provided that henceforth people gathered along the route of a royal procession shall not be chased away, but all householders shall be permitted before the sight of His Majesty, so that he may speak to those he knows and gladden their hearts."

Outside the French embassy, I occasionally discern the spectral outlines of a French gunboat, which brazenly anchored there in 1893 and proceeded to bully the Thais into parting with a substantial part of what is now Laos. Nor was this the only affront during those tense days: the crew of the ship shocked Thai sensibilities by taking their daily bath in the river stark naked, a spectacle that so incensed one elder prince that he organized a crew of swimmers to blow up the ship, and might have succeeded if King Rama V had not gotten wind of the plot and stopped it.

The riverside terrace of the Oriental Hotel, next door, is teeming with ghosts. That slightly sinister man in (I imagine) quite unsuitable dress for the tropics is possibly a certain Count Zalata, who was expelled from the Ukraine on a charge of raping seventy-two peasant girls; of this crime, Chekhov is supposed to have commented, "The man was obviously in training for something, but for what?"

Sitting not far away and looking distinctly unwell is Somerset Maugham, balancing a notebook on his knees; recovering from a near-fatal bout of malaria, he spent many days on the terrace, writing a fable about Siam entitled *Princess September*, before boarding a freighter for Cambodia. Noel Coward lounges in another deck chair, happy to be back on the river after previously trying a "beastly" hotel elsewhere in the city. "There is a terrace overlooking the swift river," he wrote in his journal, "where we have drinks every evening watching the liver-coloured water swirling by and tiny steam tugs hauling rows of barges up river against the tide. It's a lovely place and I am fonder of it than ever."

(This may be the place to note that I am not the only one to encounter ghosts along the Chao Phraya. Patrick Campbell, then columnist for the London *Sunday Times*, was once staying in the Noel

Coward Suite of the Oriental when he heard a hubbub in the garden below. Looking out he saw "a horde of foreigners, looking lumpish and hot in their Western clothes", scrambling over one another to take pictures of some beautiful girls performing the Thai classical dance. "Beside me," he wrote later, "I felt the Master humming in that light tenor voice: In Bangkok/At twelve o'clock/They foam at the mouth and run.")

Once on that terrace, I also fancied I heard the roar of engines, and past me flew a seaplane, heading for a terminal a bit further upstream. When the hotel launch returned later with the day's collection of adventurous early air travellers, who should be among them but swashbuckling Douglas Fairbanks. He was then known as the King of Hollywood, and during his stay, he informed the press, he hoped to meet the King of Siam.

I can go much further back into history, for an even more romantic trove, if I make an excursion to the old capital of Ayutthaya, which like Bangkok was also dominated by the Chao Phraya. For a few years, I had a riverside house here among the haunted ruins of temples and palaces, right on the spot (at least according to local legend) occupied by the residence of a famous seventeenth-century adventurer named Constantine Phaulkon. Greek by birth, he had a brief but dazzling career in which he rose to be one of the most powerful men at the court of King Narai; his prominence, as well as his suspected French sympathies, incurred the envy of conservative elements and following a palace revolution in 1688 he was arrested and beheaded.

I used to come across shards of blue-and-white Chinese porcelain while digging in my vegetable garden, and sometimes I thought I heard the voice of Phaulkon's part-Japanese wife, scolding the servants for breaking yet another dish. She was Catholic—supposedly, her forebears had come to Ayutthaya to escape religious persecution in Japan—and, by a rare stroke of luck, she and her son were spared in the events of 1688; indeed, her great-granddaughter was one of my Bangkok ghosts, since she became the wife of Robert Hunter.

From my verandah in Ayutthaya, as the late afternoon sunlight played luminous golden tricks on the swiftly moving waters of the river, I often observed the splendid barges carrying the first of two grand embassies from Louis XIV to King Narai on an October day in 1685. Sitting erect in one was the Chevalier de Chaumont, a rather formidable figure, looking a bit exhausted after a journey that had taken more than two hundred days but with the bright, almost feverish eyes of a true zealot; his principal aim, never to be realized, was the conversion of Narai to Christianity. Near him was his deputy, the Abbé de Choisy, sharp-eyed, too, but hardly a fanatic despite his priestly garb; he, I fancied, languidly trailed an elegant hand in the water, perhaps meditating on an exotic period in his youth when he had been a prominent transvestite in Parisian society, known as Madame de Sancy.

And beside me in the gathering darkness Phaulkon would sometimes materialize to gaze upon this exotic sight, flushed with the apparent success of his scheming, doubtless dreaming of a glorious period of Franco-Thai relations (of which he would be a prominent beneficiary), unaware that it would lead directly to the cold glint of an executioner's sword in less than three years.

So it goes. Fascinating as the Chao Phraya is on its own contemporary terms—and much of the river activity remains remarkably as it was in descriptions of a century ago—it becomes infinitely more so for me as I move among my ghostly cast of characters and watch them re-enact their long ago roles. Others, I am sure, are waiting in the wings. There is that ramshackle old palace, for instance, that I pass every time I go to a certain popular riverside restaurant. It is supposedly deserted, but through the lopsided windows I catch glimpses of pale faces peering out hopefully, pleading to be summoned back—and they will be, as soon as I can unravel their history.

7

HOBSON-JOBSON: THE PERFECT BEDSIDE BOOK

For a long time, the place of honour on my bedside table has been occupied by a weighty, densely printed volume with the intriguing title of *Hobson-Jobson*. I can think of few other books so ideally designed for soothing sleepless nights with a mixture of information, provocation, and splendid eccentricity, all presented with wit and style.

Accurately, if not concisely, subtitled *A Glossary of Colloquial Anglo-Indian Words and Phrases, and of Kindred Terms, Etymological, Historical, Geographical, and Discursive*, the work was first published in England in 1886 as a collaborative effort between Colonel Henry Yule, R.E., C.B., and A.C. Burnell, Ph.D. C.I.E. Yule, who later became Sir Henry, and Burnell, a scholarly member of the Madras Civil Service, had met by chance in London a decade or so earlier and had discovered they shared a common interest in various Indian words that had gradually insinuated themselves into the English language since Elizabethan times. Comparing notes, they decided to compile a glossary.

Burnell died shortly before the book came out, and it was left to his co-author to write the introduction. "My first endeavour in preparing this work," he noted, "has been to make it accurate; my next— even though a Glossary—interesting." Not being an etymologist, I can only assume, from the impressive display of scholarship, that he succeeded in the first aim; I know from my own experience that he did in the second. Rarely do I dip into my *Hobson-Jobson* without discovering some arresting new tidbit of unexpected information.

For Yule and Burnell were clearly preoccupied by far more than mere derivations. As the subtitle suggests, they were also avid collectors of odd facts that were frequently only distantly related to the word or phrase under discussion. And they did not hestiate to range far afield in order to display their vast knowledge of Asian exotica.

Take, for instance, the familiar word "curry". The authors start out tamely enough with a simple, no-nonsense definition—"It consists of meat, fish, fruit, or vegetables, cooked with a quantity of bruised spices and tumeric; and a little of this gives a flavour to a large mess of rice"—and note that the word comes from the Tamil *kari*, meaning "sauce". Having got these necessities out of the way, they then begin to spread their wings.

We are treated to a discussion of the similarities between Indian curry and certain dishes in Persia, Algeria, and Egypt but cautioned that, despite the resemblance, these dishes may well have been inspired not by India but "by the spiced cookery of medieval Europe and Western Asia", the former having even been coloured like curry through the use of saffron and sandalwood. Along the way, they drop in the information that "there is hardly room for doubt that capsicum or red pepper was introduced into India by the Portuguese", citing as evidence the fact that Sanskrit cookbooks, "which cannot be of any considerable antiquity", contain many recipes for curry without this now-essential ingredient.

Following a full page of discussion in this discursive manner—during which they drag in the Dutch and the Chinese—the authors offer a dozen or so quotations in which the word or some version of it appears. These start with a 1502 entry about Vasco da Gama (an "odious ruffian"), who supposedly chopped off the hands and ears of dissident Indians and sent the collection back to their ruler with instructions to make a curry of it. The last is an 1874 quote from *Blackwood's Magazine*: "The craving of the day is for quasi-intellectual food, not less highly peppered than the curries which gratify the faded stomach of a returned Nabob."

"Nabob", originally applied to an agent or delegate of some supreme chief, was long one of the most popular Anglo-Indian imports. From around the eighteenth century on, it was used to describe those Englishmen who had returned with fortunes from the East. A few nabobs probably still survive, but they, along with the word, will doubtless soon vanish as completely as the Raj that produced them.

That fate has already overtaken the colourful expression Yule chose for his title. Toward the end of the nineteenth century, though, it was commonly used by British soldiers to mean "a native festal excitement", and it offered an excellent opportunity for the authors to demonstrate their erudition. They note that it is "in fact an Anglo-Saxon version of the wailings of Mahommedans as they beat their breasts in the procession of Moharram", and then proceed to track it down through such variations as Hussan Hussain, Hossein Jossen, Jaksom Backsom, and, finally, Hobson-Jobson.

But countless other words of certain or probable Indian origin are anything but obsolete today. In some cases the route to English was a circuitous one—via a Portuguese corruption of a native word, for instance—while in others the word was adopted with little or no change. Besides curry, there are calico, chintz, and gingham; bungalow and verandah; and tomtom, tank, teak, and (probably) typhoon; along with shawl, amok, monsoon, pagoda, loot, bamboo, bangle, bazaar, and the boats called cutters and dinghies.

Yule and Burnell clearly relished controversy, and nothing pleased them more than correcting what they regarded as a misunderstanding on the part of other scholars. A fine specimen of this argumentative flourish is to be found in an entry under "dam" ("originally an actual copper coin . . . the fortieth part of a rupee"), when they launch into a discussion of the phrase "I don't give a damn". This, they believe, is plainly derived from "I don't give a dam", the original coin being of practically no value. "Whatever profanity there may be in the animus," they tartly conclude, "there is none in the etymology." It is unlikely that anyone in Hollywood had a copy of *Hobson-Jobson* back in 1939, but it might have simplified the task of David O. Selznick during the months it took him to persuade the censors to allow Rhett Butler to utter the immortal line at the end of *Gone With The Wind*.

Fascinating and useful as all these derivations are, however, the real pleasure of *Hobson-Jobson* for me lies in the magpie collection of queer facts and quotations that the two scholars assembled over their years in the East. The three pages on "mango"—one of the longest entries—are filled with oddities that have little to do with its derivation from the Tamil *man-gay*. We learn (or at least I learned) that the fruit of the wild tree is inedible (but who first produced edible hybrids?); that Alexander the Great's army got dysentery from eating too many mangoes in nothern India; that a fourteenth-century European traveller thought the mango better than a peach; and that the mango-bird, which is "a beautiful golden oriole", appears in the orchards about the time the fruit ripens.

Most of all I enjoyed the accounts of the celebrated mango trick, in the course of which a mango seed is placed under a basket and, at intervals, is revealed to have produced leaves, flowers, and finally fruit—all in under half an hour. The authors quote from several eyewitness descriptions of this stunt, my favourite being one by the Emperor Jahangir in the early seventeenth century. According to his autobiography, the ruler once beheld the miraculous growth not only of a mango but also of an apple, a fig, an almond, and a walnut tree. Nor did the trick end with the appearance of fruit of rare quality: "Before the trees were removed there appeared among the foliage birds of such surpassing beauty, in colour and shape and melody, as the world never saw before . . . . At the close of the operation, the foliage, as in the autumn, was seen to put on its variegated tints, and the trees gradually disappeared into the earth."

Hobson-Jobson has been through several editions, with certain minor corrections and additions made in the one published in 1903. Basically, though, it has remained the same and has stood the test of time amazingly well, both as a reference work and as entertainment.

It has acquired one quality, though, that may not have been anticipated by the authors: it has become a sort of nostalgic showcase for a number of words that now conjure up a whole bygone era from the pages of Kipling and Maugham and Conrad.

Who nowadays dons a solar topee, that splendid helmet that sheltered generations of mad Englishmen from the pitiless midday sun? Who sits on a bungalow veranda puffing a cheroot (cigar) after a sumptuous tiffin (lunch) before lowering the chicks (split-bamboo blinds) for a siesta? Who summons his syce (driver) and tonga (two-wheeled cart) for an evening at the club? Who, for that matter, accepts as nothing less than his due the title sahib—"by which, all over India, European gentlemen, and it may be said Europeans generally, are addressed, and spoken of, when no disrespect is intended, by natives."

I came across the most nostalgic of all words in *Hobson-Jobson* by chance one night when a chorus of bullfrogs in my flooded Bangkok garden kept me from sleeping. Idly reading through the 'h's', I was stopped abruptly by the entry "home". Surely, I thought, that cannot be derived from Hindi or Sanskrit, Tamil or Malay.

It was not. "In Anglo-Indian and colonial speech," say Yule and Burnell, "this means England."

8

THE QUEEN WHO CAME FOR DINNER

Not far from the former palace housing the Ministry of Foreign Affairs in Bangkok, overlooking one of the few canals that still run through the city, stands an enormous statue of a pig. Countless Thais, mostly women, know it as Chao Mae Moo, "The Divine Pig", and come daily to lay fragrant jasmine wreaths and apply bits of gold leaf to its ample sides. They hope by such means to have their wishes granted by the powerful spirit believed to inhabit the figure.

Yet despite its popularity, few of the pig's devotees know how it happened to be put there in the early years of the present century. They are unaware that it honours Queen Saowapa Pongsi, one of the most remarkable women in modern Thai history. Rarely seen by the general public during her lifetime and largely forgotten today except as a name that appears on a few buildings, she nevertheless played a major role in freeing her sex from centuries of ill-treatment.

The choice of animal was astrological—a reminder that the favourite wife of His Majesty King Chulalongkorn the Great was born on 1 January 1863, the day of the Waning Moon in the Year of the Pig. She was the sixty-sixth child of King Rama IV, inadequately known to the West as the hero of *The King and I*, and most of her life was spent in a world that seems as remote as the Middle Ages, though it ceased to exist only some eighty years ago.

This world was the innermost part of the Grand Palace, an incredible city-within-a-city inhabited by thousands of women and a single man. Anna Leonowens, the laundered heroine of *The King and I*, who was never one to miss a melodramatic phrase, called it "The City of Veiled Woman". She claimed that its population numbered around 9,000 during the time she taught there from 1862 to 1867. In fact, the real figure was probably around 3,000, but even that was impressive for one closely-guarded section of the mile-square palace compound.

The "Inside", as the women's quarter was known, was protected by three different walls, each with formidable gates. Since the king's wives were symbols of his mystical semi-divine powers—as were the white elephants discovered during his reign—the section had been part of the original palace design in 1782, copied after the royal residence in the former capital of Ayutthaya. By the time of Saowapa's birth, however, it had changed considerably. During the reign of King Rama II, most of the old wooden buildings had been replaced by solid, Western-style structures in brick and stucco. According to one Thai scholar, the newer buildings resembled "in a remarkable manner such houses in the Winter Palace of Imperial Peking", though he cautions, "there is no record of them being modelled on them."

Today the Inside—still out of bounds for most visitors—is a slightly eerie ghost town, deserted except for a few gardeners, some elderly female servants, and, in one area, students attending a school started by a daughter of the present King. Fading, pastel-coloured palaces, some of considerable size, line the silent streets, which also contain shuttered shops and markets. The gardens are overgrown in places; though a little waterfall still spills down an artificial hill into a jungly pool, the nearby grotto has been taken over by spooky bats and lizards.

It was all very different when Saowapa was growing up. Although King Rama IV did not begin the polygamous life expected of a ruler until he was forty-seven, he made up for lost time and eventually had a total of eighty-two children, whose mothers were given special status. There were also a number of minor wives who, for one reason or another, were not blessed with royal issue. Higher-ranking wives—and rank was a very complex issue, largely based on the ruler's personal preferences—had palaces of their own and retinues of 200–300 people. Even lesser wives had sizeable household staffs, which were substantially increased if they became mothers.

In addition, there were women shopkeepers, speciality cooks, and dressmakers to cater to the needs of the Inside, as well as a female judiciary and a much-feared female police force known as the *Krom Klone*. Dressed in blue pantaloon-like garments and white jackets with a cream-coloured scarf across the breast, the *Krom Klone* kept order and prevented outsiders from entering the great gates.

None of the wives could leave without permission of the *Atibodhi Fai Nai*, "Directress of the Inside". On the rare occasions when they did leave, they were accompanied by one or more chaperones who watched them like hawks. Male children were separated from their mothers when they reached puberty, celebrated with an elaborate Brahmin ritual during which the top-knot was cut with ceremonial scissors. Only a male who happened to become king—the one man allowed to go to the Inside at will—would ever be able to return.

Despite its restrictions, despite the fierce *Krom Klone*, most of the residents of the Inside regarded themselves as supremely fortunate to be there. For even the lowliest attendants it functioned as a kind of finishing school, training them in all sorts of domestic arts and court manners that made them much sought after as wives when they left the royal service. (Today some of their descendants are still noted for their skill at preparing certain delicacies that originated in the palace, and the exquisite floral wreaths used by the present King and Queen for various ceremonies are made daily by employees of the Inside.) And for the royal wives, aside from all the creature comforts they enjoyed, there was the ever-present possibility of attracting the king's special favour, which could bring even more glittering rewards.

Saowapa's mother had been elevated to the position of a queen and, according to Anna Leonowens, was "the only woman who ever managed the King with acknowledged success". So the little girl was automatically a member of the highest circles of the Inside, with a chief nurse, several wet nurses, and a number of maids all to herself from birth. "Never for one moment of her life was she left alone," wrote Dr. Malcolm Smith, a British physician who later attended her and became her friend and confidant.

By all accounts, she was a quick-witted child and a particular favourite of her father. According to Dr. Smith, "She played games with her brothers and sisters, but they had to be decorous ones: the rough games of the common people were not allowed. Her toilet took a long time. She was bathed, perfumed, and dressed at least twice a day, and combing, brushing, oiling, and setting of the 'top-knot' was an ordeal for her, for it took such a long time. The cutting of the top-knot when she was eleven years old was an elaborate ceremony lasting three days."

One half-brother she was probably too young to play with was Chulalongkorn, the king's eldest son, who ascended the throne in 1868 at the age of fifteen. Eleven years later, when Saowapa was sixteen, he chose her to be one of his wives, an honour also accorded to two of her sisters, Sunanta and Sawang. Some Westerners have been shocked by the idea of marriage between such close relations, and such marriages were, in fact, forbidden outside the palace. Their purpose was to maintain the purity of the royal blood, a practice which, as Dr. Smith noted, was also followed in ancient Egypt, Hawaii, Peru, and Persia.

As photographs attest, Saowapa was by no means the prettiest of the king's ninety-two wives (by whom he had seventy-seven children), nor was she the favourite—at first. That envied position was possibly held by her sister Sunanta, who suffered a uniquely tragic death in

1881 when she was barely twenty-one and pregnant. A boat carrying her to the summer palace at Bang Pa-In, just below Ayutthaya, capsized; since commoners were not allowed to touch royalty, the boatmen and spectators could only watch helplessly as she drowned.

The depth of Chulalongkorn's grief is suggested by the memorial he erected in the summer palace rose garden. It bears an inscription in both Thai and English: "To the beloved memory of her late and lamented Majesty, Sunanta Kumariratn, Queen-Consort, who was wont to spend her most pleasant and happiest hours in this garden amidst those loving ones and dearest to her. This memorial is erected by Chulalongkorn Rex, her bereaved husband, whose suffering from so cruel an endurance through those trying hours made death seem seem so near yet preferable."

But Saowapa clearly inherited many of her mother's skills, steadily advancing her position in the king's affections. Fate, which had removed Sunanta from the scene, also played a role in the question of the heir-apparent. Prince Vajiranahit, eldest son of Sawang, was proclaimed crown prince in 1885, but when he died ten years later at the age of eighteen, the succession passed to Saowapa's eldest, Vajiravudh.

Saowapa herself was then raised to the rank of "first queen", with apartments of her own in the huge, ornate, largely Western Chakri Maha Prasat that Chulalongkorn built in the Grand Palace compound. Nor was this recognition merely a matter of motherhood. As her grandson, Prince Chula Chakrabongse, has written, "With all the honours, titles, jewellery, and properties bestowed upon her, as well as apparently the greater part of his company, it would be difficult even for the prejudiced to deny that Queen Saowapa was King Chulalongkorn's most beloved wife and help-mate."

If such prejudiced souls existed—and they almost certainly did in that hotbed of palace intrigue—they received even more dramatic proof of the king's preference for Saowapa in 1897, when he became the first Thai monarch to go on a state visit to the courts of Europe. Breaking with all precedent, he appointed Saowapa as regent during his absence, giving her equal status with the ruler.

The effect on the Inside of this extraordinary step is described in *Four Reigns*, an epic novel by M. R. Kukrit Pramoj that has been translated into English. The story is told through the eyes of Ploi, a witty young girl who enters palace service during Chulalongkorn's reign and is witness to most of the major events in Thai history over the next half-century. News of the queen's appointment sets the women's world abuzz with speculation:

"How did they feel about it—the younger women of the Inner Court (and a few of the older ones, too, for that matter)? Well, what they felt had some excitement mixed in it, of course, and pride, but more pronounced than either emotion was a sense of discovery, of awakening. Ploi felt it keenly. If the Queen could become a ruler like the King, it followed then that women as human beings were on the same level as men and could step into positions usually held by men if given the opportunity. That men were lords of their households and women more or less their dependents might be the prevailing situation but by no means an unalterable one.

"She discussed it with Choi, who thoroughly agreed with her and made the following declaration to Khun Sai:

"'You know what, Khun Aunt? I'm not afraid of men anymore. I'm a woman and a woman reigns over all this land of ours.'

"'And if you don't shut up, you'll get a coconut in your mouth to shut it for you,' retorted her aunt."

By the time of her appointment as regent, Queen Saowapa had already exerted a fairly revolutionary influence through personal example alone. Perhaps because she went through the experience nine times herself, she took a particular interest in matters regarding childbirth. Traditionally, in what Dr. Smith called "a barbarous proceeding", new Thai mothers were "roasted" for a period of two to three weeks after giving birth. This unpleasant treatment consisted of placing a charcoal brazier as close to the mother's stomach as she could stand. "Often it raised huge blisters," said Dr. Smith, "and when the skin was covered with them and the patient could stick it no longer, they turned her over and blistered her back."

Saowapa decided roasting was not for her and refused to submit to it. Other wives in the palace were quick to follow her, and the practice died away, at least in the Inside.

Her interest in motherhood extended beyond the palace walls and led to the even more radical idea that Thai midwives should be sent abroad for training in modern methods of child delivery. The first step in the plan was a failure. In 1883 four girls between 10 and 12 years of age were sent to England; only after their arrival was it discovered that the English midwife schools then had a minimum age limit of 25. Undaunted, the queen donated money for a school in Bangkok, which was soon turning out hundreds of midwives.

She initiated other changes as well. Largely because of her, women of the court began to appear at public functions in the palace instead of remaining discreetly in the background. In 1908, when the Duke and Duchess of Mecklenburg paid a state visit, she was taken in for dinner at Bang Pa-In on the duke's arm, something that had never been seen before in Thailand.

Queen Saowapa accompanied the king on his frequent travels through his country. On these outlings she brought along numerous ladies from the Inside. For many it was the first time they had seen the real world and the ordinary people who inhabited it.

The queen built and endowed two girls' schools in Bangkok—another first—and four in the provinces. She founded the Thai Red Cross. When the king made the unprecedented decision to send most

of his male children abroad for their education, she strongly supported the idea over conservative opposition. One of these children scan-
dalized the court by marrying a Russian girl. Chulalongkorn adamant-
ly refused to receive the bride and stuck to the decision for the rest of
his life. Queen Saowapa, however, after registering strong initial disapproval, eventually consented to meet her and took a great liking to
her. (The prince involved, incidentally, was her second son and therefore next in line of succession after Vajiravudh. His marriage to a foreigner removed him from consideration, and the crown eventually
passed to her youngest, Prajadhipok, whose reign saw the end of the
absolute monarchy.)

When it came to certain matters, though, the queen remained a
strict traditionalist. At his coronation, Chulalongkorn had dramatically announced the end of a practice that had long drawn much criticism
from foreign observers. He told those who had come to congratulate
him: "The custom of prostration and human worship in Thailand is
manifestly an oppressive exaction which an inferior must perform to a
superior. The acts of showing honour by such prostration and worship
His Majesty perceives are of no benefit whatever to the country . . . His
Majesty proposes to substitute in place of crouching and crawling,
standing and walking; and instead of prostration on all fours and bow-
ing with palm-joined hands to the ground, a graceful bow of the head."

This decision was a body blow to the whole world in which
Saowapa had grown up, a world that regarded the king as nothing less
than the Lord of Life, and she refused to have anything to do with it.
She followed the old custom all her life, and so did most of the other
ladies of the Inside.

King Chulalongkorn died on 23 October 1910, after a reign of
forty-two years—the longest of any Thai monarch up to that time.
Queen Saowapa was devastated. For a time she continued to live in
her old quarters but eventually moved to Phya Thai Palace, a fanciful

Victorian structure on what was then the outskirts of Bangkok. There she took to her bed and rarely left it.

For the rest of the Inside, it was also the end of an era. The new king showed little interest in the vast female population of his palace, and gradually it began to disappear. The covered corridor that allowed the ruler to walk unseen from the Chakri Maha Prasat to various Inside residences rotted away, never to be replaced. Unmarried princesses moved out to assorted palaces, where they continued to be as strictly chaperoned as ever. The pleasure gardens, scene of so many happy times, succumbed to weeds.

Surrounded by her female attendants, Queen Saowapa embarked on a strange existence in which she literally turned night into day. She usually woke around sundown, had her main meal at midnight, and retired at dawn. While she slept, all traffic in the roads outside her palace was diverted, and men armed with blow pipes and clay pellets kept noisy birds out of her garden. Servants padded about on bare feet.

All visitors came at night, among them Dr. Smith, now her personal physician. "She expected a daily visit no matter what the state of her health," he wrote, "and as a confirmed valetudinarian she was never at a loss for a complaint. She had an utter belief in medicine, and a stock of tried prescriptions was always kept at hand for the relief of any symptoms that might sudenly arise. Not a day passed without some of these being taken."

In between medical matters she quizzed the doctor on European affairs, especially those involving crowned heads, about whom she had "astonishingly complete" knowledge: "She knew their family trees far better than I did, and spoke of the people almost as if they were her own relations."

She was miserable when no one came to chat with her in the small hours of the morning. Once Dr. Smith arrived to find her in tears: "She was utterly lonely (sob). All her sons had gone away and there was no one left to talk to (sob). How selfish they were, how thought-less, to leave her all alone when they knew she was so ill (sob). But the mood soon passed. Here, at any rate for the moment, was someone to talk to. She dried her tears and blew her nose, and in the music of her own voice her troubles disappeared."

Enormously wealthy in her own right, she was extremely generous to her relatives and those who attended her, as well as to the assorted schools and charities she supported. But she could be a terror in other ways, especially toward the surviving wives and daughters of the late king. As the accepted head of the family, she still had power over them and frequently used it to express unconcealed dislike. Dr. Smith records the time a group of unmarried princesses came to see her off on one of her rare excursions outside Phya Thai Palace. "Did she smile upon them as she passed by or stay a moment to chat with them as she should have done? Not a word; not a look. With a face as inscrutable as a sphinx, she walked past them."

Her sedentary life probably contributed to her relatively early death, in 1919. There was little public mourning; she had been so long out of sight that few outside of royal circles remembered her as an individual. Despite her years at Phya Thai Palace, she belonged, essentially, to the secret world of the Inside, already fading from most memories.

Today her name is perpetuated in the Saowapa Institute, where vaccines against small pox, rabies, and snake bites are produced. But her true spirit, perhaps, resides in the Divine Pig, from which it con-tinues to dole out favours to the needy and deserving.

9

CHARMED LIVES

E ven the briefest of visits to Thailand is sufficient to show the overwhelming presence of Buddhism. Glittering temples greet the eye almost everywhere, monks pad through the early morning streets to receive their daily rice from the faithful, and no young man is regarded as having attained true maturity without spending a spell in a monastery.

It takes a little longer for the visitor to perceive that Buddhism is by no means the only way Thais approach the mysteries of the spirit. Rarely discussed with outsiders, even more rarely dealt with by serious scholars, these other approaches are nonetheless a vital and enduring part of daily Thai life, influencing all levels of society from the lowest to the most sophisticated.

A foreigner's first awareness of this phenomenon often comes when he notes the charming miniature houses set atop posts in just about every compound, whether of a luxury hotel or a simple country house, decked out with fresh flowers and little figurines. Alternatively, he may be walking about Bangkok and observe great homage being paid to some plainly non-Buddhist image—a multi-armed god, perhaps, an enormous pig thickly plastered with gold leaf, or a huge and quite unmistakable phallus. Or, still again, he may notice that the gold chain most Thais wear around their necks carries an often large and clanking collection of amulets.

This initial perception is apt to be confusing, however, because many of the items mentioned above may seem directly or indirectly connected to Buddhism. The little structures are often replicas of religious buildings, the god or phallus may preside from a shrine within the precincts of a temple, and the amulets generally bear a bas-relief of the Buddha or perhaps some highly revered monk.

The truth is that in Thailand, as in Burma, Laos, and Cambodia, Theravada Buddhism coexists comfortably with an assortment of other beliefs, many of them far older and deeply ingrained in local custom. Nine centuries ago, in Burma's great capital of Pagan, King Anawrahta shrewdly installed images of the thirty-six Nats, or demigods, in his splendid Shwezigon Pagoda to encourage acceptance of the new faith he himself had adopted; and this tolerant intermingling has continued throughout all the Buddhist countries of Southeast Asia, sometimes to the point where it is hard to separate the two.

Almost no Thai male, and relatively few females, would think of venturing forth from home unguarded by some sort of magic charm, usually in the form of a small votive tablet attached to a chain. Three or four are often worn at the same time, providing different sorts of protection. One noted collector who lives just outside Bangkok claims to have more than a thousand and regularly wears several dozen. At least six Thai-language publications are devoted exclusively to amulets, offering histories of the more famous types, advice on how to distinguish the real from the bogus, and personal accounts of their powers. Customers willing to pay prices that ascend into the thousands of dollars for a prized specimen crowd Bangkok's several amulet markets.

Such enthusiasm is easy to understand after reading almost any of the amulet testimonials that appear more or less routinely in the magazines. Take, for example, the story of little five-year-old Chalermsri, who dashed across a Bangkok street and was run over by a speeding truck. Unconscious and to all appearances mortally injured, the child was rushed to a hospital. There, doctors were amazed to find she had no serious internal injuries at all. Even more startling, when they tried to give her an injection, the needle would not penetrate her skin. The reason, soon discovered, was that she was wearing a Phra Pichit Med Khao Mao, one of the most noted of amulets when it comes to protecting the wearer from physical injury.

Another account tells of a minibus driver who, stricken with all sorts of bad luck, could barely make ends meet. He invested in two famous amulets—a Phra Kring Uttama and a Phra Prok Bai Makham Uttama, each named after a venerated monk—and his fortunes immediately improved. He not only began getting customers (even when he asked more than other drivers) but was spared from thieves and accidents. As a result, all the minibus drivers in his section of the city now carry the amulets.

Even more remarkable, according to the magazines, are the Phra Rod amulets, which tradition claims were produced in northern Thailand more than a thousand years ago by a hermit named Narod. These come in five different colours, each possessing its own special powers. The white Phra Rod not only protects the wearer from a variety of harms but "arouses feelings of love, affection, and compassion in others". The green is favoured by those who have to go regularly into the jungle, since it is effective against ghosts, demons, and wild animals. The yellow promotes successful deals in the world of trade, while the red offers protection against criminals of all kinds. By far the most sought after, however, is the black; it does nothing less than "endow the wearer with invincibility".

All these amulets are little clay tablets bearing a light relief of a seated Buddha. Such tablets were originally made in India as souvenirs for pilgrims who came to the four holy places: Lumbini, where the Buddha was born; Bodh Gaya, where he attained enlightenment; Sarnath, where he preached his first sermon; and Kusinara, where he died. Later, similar ones were made for poor Buddhists who could not afford a stone or bronze image, while still others were made in large numbers and interred at the base of stupas as a form of merit making.

Precisely when or how they also acquired their magic properties is uncertain, but from the earliest days of Buddhism in Thailand monks have been closely associated with the manufacture and potency of amulets. Tablets made or blessed by venerated monks of the past are among the most valued, and word of an amulet trove found in some ancient stupa will attract a stampede of collectors from all over the country.

Not all Thai amulets are associated with Buddhism, however. Others come in a wide variety of forms, which are lumped together under the general name of *khwang khlang*, "sacred, potent objects". The Baw Paw Raw Medal, for instance—produced on the occasion of the present Thai king's forty-eighth birthday, when it was presented to policemen—has already acquired considerable renown for its protective powers.

Amulets may also be odd-shaped stones and bits of metal. One, probably from a meteorite, is called "the stone from the sky". Still others are semiprecious stones like cat's-eyes; parts of an animal, such as a boar's tusk or a tiger's tooth; and small figurines carved from the wood of certain "lucky" trees, like the sacred fig, the sandalwood, and the star gooseberry.

A rather unusual group of Thai amulets are those called *palad khik*, which can be translated as "deputy penis". Most of these phallus replicas are realistically carved from rare woods, coral, ivory, horn, or any of a number of other materials, and range in size from a few centimetres to huge specimens that some dealers, exercising a considerable degree of poetic licence, call "life size". Some more elaborate *palad khik* have legs or the figure of a woman or monkey crouched on top of them.

Relatively little research has been done on phallic amulets (one noted anthropologist apologized to his readers for even having to describe them), but it seems likely that they originated in the Hindu worship of the linga and that they entered Thai culture by way of Cambodia. Many of the most treasured bear an inscription in old Khmer script, and in former days the amulets were commonly worn by young men in Cambodia.

Palad khik are traditionally attached to a cord worn around the waist (never around the neck) and one of their basic functions apparently is to deflect possible harm from the wearer's sexual organs; hence the popular name. But they are also believed to provide protection from other dangers, as well as to bring general good luck, especially in business. More citified believers carry them in their pockets. Women, especially of the older generation, sometimes carry one in their handbags since the amulet is regarded as effective in discouraging purse snatchers.

As with the votive tablets, *palad khik* frequently derive their special powers from having been blessed by a Buddhist monk. Among the most noted priests associated with them in Thailand was one called Luang Paw Bo, whose talents allegedly included the ability to fly and to be in two places at once. *Palad khik* attributed to this unusual man are supposed to be capable of shooting upstream like a jet when placed in a river.

Amulets offer continuing protection from life's daily dangers, but when Thais are in need of some special help—a favourable response to a marriage proposal, for example, a good grade in an examination, or a winning number in the national lottery—they tend to call on one of the gods who inhabit the innumerable non-Buddhist shrines of the country.

The most common are those that house the resident spirit of each compound, a being who watches over the general welfare of the property but who can also be called on in emergencies. Sometimes simple little wooden houses—diminutive versions of the traditional Thai house—but often elaborately decorated affairs in stucco and cement, these must be kept regularly supplied with floral offerings, tidbits of food, and lighted joss sticks, as well as figurines representing human and animal attendants.

An ignored or unhappy spirit is capable of all sorts of mischief, from starting family quarrels to causing mysterious accidents or illnesses. When Jim Thompson, founder of the Thai silk industry, disappeared while on a holiday in Malaysia, the employees of his company consulted numerous seers in an effort to discover his whereabouts. One finally decided that the spirit who looked after Thompson's office building was to blame for the simple reason that it was discontented with its accommodation. Thompson, a noted collector of Asian art, had provided an antique spirit house, whereas the spirit wanted fancier quarters. The old house was replaced with a shiny new one; but either the spirit remained unmollified by the change or was blameless to begin with, for the missing man has never returned.

A happier outcome ensued in another difficult case, where the owner of a house made regular and generous offerings to his spirit yet still was plagued by mishaps. This time the experts discovered a surprising reason for the spiritual wrath: the food offering often included pork, and since the resident spirit happened for some reason to be Muslim, it was understandably offended. As soon as dietary changes were made, the difficulties abruptly ended.

Other, more public shrines also abound in Thailand and can be consulted by anyone with an urgent problem. One of the most popular is the *lak muang*, or "city pillar", which is to found in nearly every provincial capital, generally at or near the exact geographical centre of the original town. Usually a tall column with a bulbous top, the *lak muang* has long been regarded by Europeans as an obvious phallic symbol, derived like the *palad khik* from the Shiva-linga of India. But a recent study by an Australian anthropologist casts doubt on this easy assumption, noting that "what is 'obviously' a phallus in Western Europe need not necessarily be so in Thailand". Thais, the study found, tend to compare the pillar to some plant, such as a lotus bud or the tip of a banana blossom.

Phallic or not, the *lak muang* is nearly always an important centre of supplication wherever it is found. The most famous one of all, in Bangkok, was installed in 1782 by King Rama I, not far from the Grand Palace. People come to it by the thousands with offerings of gold leaf, jasmine wreaths, and incense, asking for their wishes to be granted and promising various rewards if they are—a roasted chicken, perhaps, or a pig's head, a hundred boiled eggs, a bottle of whisky, performances of classical dancing and folk opera, sometimes cash and jewellery. In 1969, the War Veterans Organization, which is responsible for management of the shrine, spent 1.6 million baht to refurbish the place and add a safety vault for the protection of the money and valuables donated by the grateful. The funds are used for maintenance and also for charity.

One Bangkok shrine that is undeniably phallic is located at the end of a narrow, tree-shaded lane near the British Embassy, Here a personal note must intrude, for back in 1963 I moved into a house with a garden that led directly into the site of this shrine, the abode of a female spirit named Chao Mae Tuptim. Though still in use, the place was in a sad state when I first saw it, half-smothered in a tangle of tropical creepers and knee-high grass. The offerings, however, were stacked everywhere—hundreds of sculptured phalluses, large and small, crude and refined, glistening with bright red paint or riddled with termites like a dreadful warning against the ravages of venereal disease.

With the encouragement of my landlady, a sophisticated woman who owned Bangkok's largest bus company, I undertook the task of clearing away the undergrowth and planting a lawn and some ornamental shrubs. Soon the shrine began attracting increasing numbers of people. Some were women seeking the birth of a child; others came to ask for a lucky lottery ticket or a successful outcome to a job application. The rate of success must have been good, for new and more elaborate offerings poured in. One consisted of a gigantic phallus supported by two life-sized legs, while another appeared in the form of a jumbo jet. Once a woman brought a large tray of freshly baked phallic buns, shocking pink in colour.

More Europeans discovered the unusual shrine, too, and over the years it acquired a certain celebrity. One of the American men's magazines devoted several pages to a colour spread of the offerings, and the final chapter of the book (though not the movie) version of *Emmanuelle* takes place there. Numerous photographers, claiming a keen interest in anthropology, came and set up their tripods.

Subsequently, my house was torn down to make way for the Hilton International Hotel. Chao Mae Tuptim's shrine was spared, though, and still attracts devotees in a corner of the hotel's large garden.

With the possible exception of *lak muang*, the most famous of all Bangkok's non-Buddhist shrines is undoubtedly the one adjacent to another hotel, the Grand Hyatt Erawan, overlooking a busy commercial intersection. Consisting of an ornate little pavilion that shelters a gilded statue of the Hindu god Brahma, this is not the hotel's spirit house (which is located elsewhere) but rather a special shrine built to meet certain extraordinary circumstances.

These occurred during construction of the original, government-owned Erawan on the site back in the 1950s, when accident after accident plagued the workers. The last straw, apparently, came when a ship bringing Italian marble for the lobby sank at sea, convincing all concerned that malign forces were at work. Since "Erawan", the name selected for the hotel, was the three-headed elephant on which Brahma traditionally rode, it seemed logical to dedicate a shrine to that particular god. After this was done in 1955, the mishaps ceased at once, and the hotel opened the following year.

Somewhat to the management's surprise, however, the shrine proved as popular with the general public as with Erawan employees. The corner became one of the liveliest places in Bangkok, especially in the early evenings, when hundreds of supplicants crowded into the compound. It has been necessary to enlarge the space several times, most recently when the old Erawan gave way to a newer, grander Grand Hyatt.

Countless wooden elephants, large and small, have been given to the spirit in thanks for assistance, so many the management has to clear them out periodically to make room for more. As he is believed to be especially fond of pretty girls, performances of folk and classical dancing are sponsored every day. Rumour has it that some women have danced bare-breasted late at night, and at least one is supposed to have done it naked in the early morning hours.

The average Thai regards it as only natural to call on every possible source of aid in times of urgent need, as was shown by a recent case involving a well-to-do lady. By accident one evening, she swallowed three needles that had been left in a pillbox on her bedside table. X-rays subsequently revealed them in her stomach, and her alarmed physician advised an immediate operation. Dreading surgery, the woman asked for three days to invoke the intercession of other powers, a request to which the doctor reluctantly agreed.

She drew first on religion, going to the renowned Temple of the Emerald Buddha, where she pledged five hundred boiled eggs to the image if he helped her with the problem. Then she went to the Erawan shrine, promising a troop of the prettiest dancing girls in the most splendid costumes. Finally, she invested in a powerful magnet, which she placed in a strategic position when she retired at night.

With such an assortment of forces working for her, the woman was scarcely surprised—though undoubtedly relieved—when the needles made a dramatic appearance on the third day. The Emerald Buddha and the Erawan spirit were promptly given their rewards. As for the magnet, which may or may not have played a part in the miracle, it was given to a nephew, who now carries it as a lucky amulet.

10

THE SURPRISING WORLD OF CAPSICUM

"I hope you don't mind food that's a little spicy," said my host, in what I subsequently looked back on as a model of understatement. It was my very first night in Bangkok, and I was about to sit down to my very first Thai meal—an unlikely situation today, forty years later, when Thai restaurants are common even in remote corners of the United States. Nevertheless, I confidently assured him that I was partial to hot foods; I had lived in Texas, home of incendiary chile con carne, and had travelled widely in Mexico where the enchiladas and *salsa cruda* (also known as Hellfire and Damnation Sauce) could hardly be called bland.

I decided to start with a creamy soup, in which floated a few delectable-looking prawns and what appeared to be a quantity of chopped chives or spring onion tops. Nothing to worry about there, I thought, and took a generous spoonful.

The effect was slightly delayed but highly dramatic when it came. Several explosions took place simultaneously in my mouth, with the cumulative effect of a small atomic bomb. I gasped and turned beet-red, sweat suddenly pouring down my face; in blind panic I reached for the nearest glass of cool water.

My host looked up with mild concern but no great surprise. "Oh dear," he remarked. "You must have gotten one of the little ones. They're exceptionally hot."

The cause of my discomfort, of course, was a tiny green chilli, one of numerous varieties with which the Thais liberally lace many of their favourite dishes. Similar peppers, of varying degrees of potency, are also integral to the cuisines of nearly every other Asian country, from India to China, to such an extent that most people probably assume they have always been around in the region. I assumed so, too, until I did a little research and came up with some surprising discoveries.

In fact, there is no mention of the chilli pepper in either ancient Sanskrit or Chinese, nor for that matter in Latin, Greek, or Hebrew. The reason is simple: the huge genus *Capiscum*, to which all peppers belong, is native to Mexico and South America and remained unknown to the world at large until Columbus made his great voyage of discovery in 1492.

Within their original confines, though, capsicums go far back beyond recorded history. The earliest known evidence of their existence comes from the desert valley of Tehuacan, some 150 miles south of Mexico city, where archaeological finds show they were part of native diet as long ago as 7000 B.C. These were very likely some of the twenty-odd wild capsicums that have been identified, shrubby, perennial plants some two to six feet high on which the small, pungent fruits generally grow erect. At some point between 5200 and 3400 B.C., the Indians of Mexico learned through a process of selection to cultivate varieties on which the fruits were pendulant, making them less susceptible to damage from birds and also much more varied in colour, shape, flavour, and size. Peppers were thus among the first plants to be domesticated in the Americas, along with maize, beans, and squash.

Columbus' principal motive in setting forth on his expedition was to discover the source of exotic Oriental spices craved by Europeans to enliven their bland food. He was particularly eager to find a supply of black pepper, which at the time came overland by slow-moving Arab caravans, acquiring such value over the long journey that its cost soared and it was literally counted out, peppercorn by peppercorn, when it finally reached its destination.

The explorer, as everyone knows, found neither Asia nor black pepper. He did, however, observe that the natives of the West Indies were using a highly-flavoured little fruit to season their food, and he referred to it in the first letter he wrote back to his sponsors, King Ferdinand and Queen Isabella: "In these islands there are mountains where the cold this winter was very severe but the people endure it from habit and with the aid of the meat they eat with very hot spices."

As subsequent explorations revealed, the practice was not confined to chilly mountainous regions. The Spaniards who conquered Mexico noted that the Aztec aristocracy enjoyed such delicacies as frog with green chillis, tadpole with small chillis, and newt with yellow chillies, and peppers were equally ubiquitous in the food of ordinary citizens. Pizarro found them popular with the Incas of Peru, as did the Portuguese with the natives of Brazil.

The West Indians, in their now-extinct language, called the capsicum fruit *axi*, which in their reports the Spaniards rendered as *aji* or *agi*; the name chilli came from Nahuatl, the language of the Aztecs, and later entered English either in that form or in such variant spellings as chillie, chilly, chili, and chile, all referring to the hot varieties rather than to the mild or "sweet" forms like the so-called bell pepper. Columbus, seeking to identify the new spice with an older one, called it pimento, after *pimenta*, the Spanish word for black pepper, thereby initiating a degree of confusion that has prevailed in many languages ever since. The botanical name is of uncertain derivation; some claim it stems from the Latin *capsula*, meaning chest or box, in reference to its shape, while others believe its origin is the Greek *kaptain* or *kapto*, meaning "to bite".

Capsicum seeds have a viability of several years, are easily transported, and find hospitable growing conditions almost everywhere. For these reasons, probably no other spice in history spread so rapidly from its native habitat, by so many circuitous routes. Among the first to reach Spain were sent by priests who accompanied the explorers and conquistadors. They were planted in monastery gardens—not, however, for the purpose of seasoning food but for the ornamental appeal of their small bright-red fruits. The real use of capsicums as a spice and foodstuff in Europe began in the sixteenth century, when the Ottoman Turks brought them to the Balkan peninsula, from which they soon found their way throughout the continent.

No definite proof exists, but it seems likely that peppers reached India with the Portuguese, who probably brought them from Brazil or Portugal itself. Other traders then spread them to the rest of Asia, where their pungent bite became such a popular addition to local dishes that their foreign origin was soon forgotten. (The same thing happened with many ornamental plants of New World origin, among them the Bougainvillea, the Allamanda, and the Plumeria, or Frangipani.) The English, for example, got their first capsicums from India, around the middle of the sixteenth century; when they crossed the Atlantic to establish a new colony, they carried seeds with them and this reintroduced it to America.

Today, just about every language in the world contains at least one word for both sweet and hot peppers. To mention but a few, in Arabic it is *filfile*, in Russian *struchkovy*, in French *piment de Guinée*, in Hungarian *paprika*, in Swahili *piri-piri*, in Japanese *togarashi*, in Chinese *la-chio*. The little bombshell that laid me low in Bangkok, I learned, was called *prik-kee-noo*, which translates into English, rather unappetizingly, as "rat-dropping pepper".

More often than not, the language contains a great variety of names, for capsicums are prodigious hybridizers and unless carefully controlled develop countless local forms. In Thailand, for instance, there are 135 recognized types, and in Mexico the number is believed to be around 200, though no one seems to be quite sure.

Despite this bewildering diversity, however, not only of names but also of size, shape, flavour, and degree of pungency, all the world's pepper cultivars derive from only five domesticated species, and none differ greatly from those grown by the Indians of pre-Columbian Mexico and South America. The great majority, in fact, belong to a single species, *Capsicum annum*, which encompasses a range that extends all the way from the mild bell pepper to the fiery Jalapeno and *prik-kee-noo*.

Methods of cultivating capsicums vary with species and locale, but generally the slow-germinating seeds are grown first in flats or greenhouses and then transplanted when the seedlings are about six inches tall. For best results, the field should be in the full sun and the soil well-drained. Leaf colour ranges through various shades of green on most types, though some are purple; similarly the flowers vary in colour, with cream or white being the most common. As a rule, the hotter the pepper the smaller the leaves on the plant that bears it.

Green capsicums are ready for harvesting two to three months after germination and the fully mature red pods after around 130 days. The average yield on peppers is one pound per plant, though this depends on a number of factors like weather and the amount of fertilizer used. In most parts of the world, peppers are harvested by hand and then either sent fresh for sale in the market or else dried in the sun or by artificial heat.

Capsicum's varied uses as condiment, spice, and vegetable have ensured it a prominent place in cooking throughout the world. It is the principal ingredient in all curry powders, whether bought ready-made from a supermarket or carefully blended by hand in the traditional Indian fashion. Pizza parlours from New York to Singapore offer dried flakes of the milder styles as a standard condiment. Few kitchen spice racks would be complete without a jar of cayenne, as ground red pepper is often called, as well as one of paprika, the basic seasoning of Hungarian cuisine. Pepper sauces in countless variations, succulent pimentos, and pickled pepper also turn up nearly everywhere.

For years, the average Westerner thought of Chinese food almost exclusively in terms of bland Cantonese fare. The discovery of Szechuan cooking, with its lavish use of hot peppers, thus came as something of a revelation, apparently a welcome one. Koreans are enthusiastic users, too, especially in *kimchi*, the powerful blend of pickled cabbage, red pepper, and garlic that accompanies every meal.

Nor is the use of capsicum confined to making food taste better. In the Chinese province of Kueichew, women claim the thickness of their hair is due to a pepper diet. Thais believe that an occasional hot chilli makes a pet mynah bird speak more fluently, and studies have suggested that chickens grow faster when fed red peppers. Deep-heat liniment, widely used by athletes for rubdowns, contains oleoresin extracted from capsicums. Peppers in highly concentrated form are a chief ingredient in Mace, the aerosol spray popular for warding off attackers, and several preparations to stop children from sucking their thumbs are pepper-based; New York authorities reportedly put chilli powder in subway token slots in an effort to stop juvenile delinquents who were sucking the tokens out. A homemade insect spray for organic gardeners consists of cayenne pepper, garlic, onions, soap flakes, and water, while crushed chillis applied to a flower bed will supposedly discourage squirrels from eating bulbs. Finally, carotenoids, another capsicum extract, are used to give food products, drugs, and cosmetics a more appealing colour.

In the United States, the most popular capsicum is undoubtedly the bell type, of which some 111 different kinds are listed in seed catalogues. Americans are increasingly developing a taste for hotter peppers, though, as evidenced by the remarkable growth of the so-called Tex-Mex food industry. The first half of the name is justified, for though Tex-Mex certainly has a Mexican ancestry, many of its favourite creations originated north of the border. Chilli powder, for instance, a mixture of garlic powder, oregano, cumin, cayenne, and paprika, is not, as many believe, an ancient Aztec concoction; it was devised by a German resident of Texas named Willie Gebhardt in 1892. Similarly, the celebrated chile con carne was born only in the early nineteenth century in the Texas city of San Antonio.

The American hot-pepper craze is clearly more than a passing fad. A group of fanciers in Las Cruces, New Mexico, formed a club called the International Connoisseurs of Green and Red Chile as something of a joke. Nevertheless, it soon had eleven chapters (called pods) in the U.S. and one abroad, with a membership of about 3,000, and began publishing a quarterly bulletin entitled *The Chile Connoisseur News*.

Another stunt that unexpectedly turned into a national event was one organized by Frank Xavier Tolbert, a columnist on the *Dallas Morning News* who also founded the Chile Appreciation Society. Tolbert's passion for chile con carne led him to organize the Wick Fowler Memorial World Championship Chile Cookoff, named after a noted chile cook, in the tiny town of Terlingua, Texas, in 1967. Within a few years, the event was attracting about 8,000 chile buffs from all over America and also from foreign countries. (A Southeast Asian Chile Cookoff was held in the late 1970s at the home of the *Time* magazine correspondent and drew about fifteen contestants.)

Enthusiasts like to exchange stories of capsicums that have achieved immortality of one kind or another. For instance, there was the pepper that played a major role in the 1937 Nobel Prize for physiology and medicine. The award was made to Albert Szent-Gyorgyi, a Hungarian scientist, for his discovery of ascorbic acid, better known as vitamin C. During the years of his experimentation, Szent-Gyorgyi tried numerous ways to obtain enough of the acid for proper chemical analysis, but the amount was always insufficient. The great breakthrough came by accident one night when his wife happened to prepare a traditional dish of sweet peppers, or paprika as they are called in Hungary.

Unlike the great majority of his countrymen, Szent-Gyorgyi was not overly fond of paprika, so instead of eating them he took the dish to his laboratory. "By midnight that night," he later said, "I knew I had a treasure trove." Peppers proved such a rich source of vitamin C that within a month he was able to prepare three pounds of ascorbic acid to send to scientific colleagues in other countries; before the year was out the chemical structure of the substance was ascertained, making artificial production possible.

Then there was the legendary pepper upon which a remarkable industry was founded. Though there is a Mexican state called Tabasco, no pepper by that name is recorded in the early history of the country. Its first appearance, in a variant spelling, came shortly before the American Civil War, in New Orleans, when a local newspaper credited a man named Maunsell White with introducing "Tobasco red pepper", though where he obtained it was unexplained. A few years later, White was advertising something described as "Extract of Tobasco Pepper".

Some time before the war started, White gave some pods of the mysterious pepper to his friend Edmund McIlhenny, who lived with his wife on a plantation outside New Orleans called Avery Island. The McIlhennys were forced to flee during the conflict, and when they returned in 1865 the place was in ruins. In the kitchen garden, though, a few of the plants grown from White's seeds still flourished, and it was from these that McIlhenny produced a fermented pepper sauce that went on the market in 1869.

The sauce has been the subject of several lawsuits over the years, and in one of them the founder's son offered this account of how it got its famous name: "The man who had given him the pepper originally told him that he had, just prior to giving him the pepper, been in the Republic of Mexico and in the state of Tabasco. My father, after discussing other names, decided to give the name 'tabasco' to this sauce, because it was a euphonious name."

Today there are several hot sauces based on the pepper but only one that can be legally called Tabasco Pepper Sauce. The company is still family-owned, still based on Avery Island (although it has other plantations in Mexico and South America), and each year the president still pays a ceremonial visit to the fields to select plants for seed propagation, as insurance against contamination by outside strains.

And, finally, there was the first Capsicum in space. In November of 1982, astronaut Bill Lenoir took a bag of fresh Jalapenos—the favorite hot pepper among U. S. aficionados—when he went into orbit aboard the spaceship Columbia.

Aside from such achievements, peppers have been the subject of a considerable amount of scientific research. The question of what makes them so hot was answered in 1877, when an Englishman working in India first crystallized the substance known as capsaicin. Another scientist who later worked on its chemical structure wrote, "The enormous pungency of capsaicin can be appreciated only by those who have been brought into intimate contact with it." By way of proof, he offered the discovery that "a drop of a solution containing one part in 100,000 causes a persistent burning on the tongue. A drop of a solution of one part to a million imparts a pereptible warmth."

Among laymen, there seems to be a degree of misunderstanding about exactly which parts of a pepper are the hottest. Many cookbooks, for example, warn the reader to remove the seeds in order to reduce the heat of the resulting dish. Actually, research has shown that there is little capsaicin in the seeds, most of it being concentrated in the placenta, or ribs, that divide the pepper interior into sections.

Moreover, the capsaicin content can vary widely, not only among plants of the same species but even in the fruit of a single plant. In general, plants grown in hot countries have more capsaicin that those cultivated in cold; even in a temperate place, a heat wave will increase the pungency.

Heat in peppers is measured by the Scoville Organoleptic Test. Devised in 1912, this has a number of limitations, one of them being that humans are used as a taste panel and the results could be distorted if a true chilli addict slipped into the group—a character, say, like the man identified only as "Smoky Joe", who allegedly set a world record for pepper eating at a contest when he slowly munched 115 japalenos without ill effect. Nevertheless, the test has produced some rough figures that are useful for purposes of comparison. In bell peppers, for instance, the number of Scoville Heat Units is zero, while in a jalapeno it ranges from 2,500 to 4,000; in a tabasco pepper it soars to between 60,000 and 80,000, perhaps enough to give even Smoky Joe pause for thought.

Research has been done, too, on the effects of peppers on the body, suggesting that there may be considerable truth in the oft-noted paradox that "hot foods make you cool". A 1954 study required stalwart subjects to chew chilli peppers for about five minutes and found they experienced "marked salivation accompanied by varying degrees of crying and nasal discharge along with sweating, which is always confined to the face and scalp". Since evaporation of perspiration has a cooling effect, the subjects did indeed feel a difference.

Peppers contain twice as much vitamin C as citrus fruits and they are also rich in vitamins A, E, and P. An early Spanish writer, Father Jose de Acosta, claimed that capsicum was "prejudiciall to the health of young folks, chiefly to the soule, for it provokes to lust". Medical science fails to support this belief, but later studies do confirm his contention that "taken moderately, it helps and comforts the stomack for digestion", by stimulating the mucous membrane of the stomach.

After absorbing all this information, most of it new to me, I decided to investigate the local situation a little more. Any Thai market, I discovered, offers a broad range of bright red and green peppers, art-

fully arranged in bamboo baskets. The most popular are the fiery little *prik-kee-noos*, which Thai chilli connoisseurs swear are hotter than
anything Mexico has to offer. Close rivals are *prik-chee-fa*, "the pepper that points to the sky", so called because the fruits grow erect, and
prik-man, "shiny pepper", esteemed for the satiny appearance of its
skin. In addition, there are other varieties with equally expressive
names—*prik-pla-lai*, "eel intestines", *prik-duae-kai*, "fighting cock's
spur", and *prik-nau-nang*, "maiden's finger".

Certain provinces of Thailand are noted for the quality of the peppers grown in them. One is Ratchaburi, south of Bangkok, and I drove
down there for a look at commercial capsicum cultivation.

There was no problem locating a farm. Not far from Damnern
Saduak, a popular tourist centre because of its daily floating market,
they lined both sides of the road, each a neat acre or so of pepper
plants in raised beds with irrigation ditches in between. Picking one at
random, we got out and walked along a high dyke to a field where several young girls in blue cotton jackets and broad-brimmed straw hats
were weeding. The plants were about two feet tall, with dark-green
leaves; white flowers bloomed on some and as I drew closer I could
see the glossy green fruit hanging down like small fingers.

"*Prik-man*," said the friend who accompanied me, glancing at the
field with a practised eye. "Not so hot but very popular as a garnish."

A field not far away was devoted to *prik-chee-fa*, with little red, yellow, and green chillies pointing upwards like Christmas-tree lights,
and another was planted solely with *prik-kee-noo*, the quarter-inch
bombshells that separate the men from the boys—or, perhaps more
accurately, the natives from the tourists.

The separation of the varieties into different fields reduces the
danger of cross-hybridization, but according to the workers all have
more or less the same growing habits. Seeds of the desired species,
carefully culled from plants of proven quality, are sown in well-

manured soil. The plants start bearing when they are about three months old, the fruit green at first and then turning red in some cases after some fifteen days. Thais like both red and green, and shades of yellow-orange in between, so the plants can be harvested almost continuously once they start bearing. Around seven to eight months from the time of planting, fruit production slows and the field is ready for a new crop.

While we were looking over the fields, the workers had been following us, apparently fascinated by the spectacle of a *farang* who wanted to see how *prik-kee-nu* grew. From time to time they whispered together, and at last one summoned up the courage to come near. She pointed to a chilli-laden plant and said, between irrepressible giggles, "You like?"

As I nodded, memories of that first Thai meal came flooding back. Memories, too, of something else the sixteenth-century Father Acosta had written about what he called "the naturall spice that God hath given to the West Indies" on the other side of the world. No doubt after trying some axi himself, he noted that "it is mockery to say that it is not hote, it is so in the highest degree".

So when the girl, deciding to call my bluff, picked a few chillies and handed them to me, I'm afraid I proved to be a spoil-sport. Instead of emulating Smoky Joe right there in the pepper fields of Ratchaburi, I wrapped them carefully in a handkerchief and said I'd have them with my dinner that evening.

And so I did. I can't be sure, of course, but I'd estimate they came out at about 70,000 on the Scoville Heat Unit scale.

11

BELOVED AND REVILED: THE LEGENDARY DURIAN

S ooner or later, if you live in Southeast Asia, you'll come into contact with a durian. My encounter came quite early, when I was
invited to have dinner with a Thai friend who lived across the
river from Bangkok in the neighbouring community of Thonburi. I
went by boat through a network of *klongs*, which in those days thread-
ed through a semi-rural landscape of fruit orchards and vegetable
farms, and it was during the journey that I caught my first whiff of a
strange, potent odour drifting across the water.

Novice that I was, I initially thought I was smelling the water itself,
for it was the hot season and the *klongs* were low and murky.
Gradually, though, I realized that it emanated from something quite
distinct and that it was highly individual in character. "Like a rotten
onion" was the comparison made by a seventeenth-century visitor
from Europe; another was reminded of "a mixture of old cheese and
onions, flavored with turpentine"; while a third described it as being
reminiscent of "exceedingly defective sanitation".

Even on that first encounter, my own judgment was less harsh.
(Today, I greet the aroma's annual appearance with all the eagerness
of an English gardener awaiting the first waft of lilac.) It was strong,
certainly, with a powerful suggestion of sulphur, but I found it odd
rather than actively offensive and thus unknowingly placed myself in
a very small minority group of Westerners.

The smell positively assailed me when I left the boat and walked a
short distance through an orchard to my friend's house; and there,

prominently displayed on a low table in the sitting room, I found one of the sources. It was a huge fruit, shaped somewhat like an American football and covered with lethal-looking green spines that gave it the appearance of a medieval weapon. A segment of the formidable armour had been carefully cut away, revealing a meaty wedge of creamy-yellow pulp set like a rare jewel inside.

"Durian," said my friend. "The greatest fruit in the world."

All over Southeast Asia, millions echo this enthusiastic endorsement of the produce of *Durio zibethinus*, as the tree is known to botanists. Much as they esteem the succulent mango, the delicate rambutan, and the versatile guava, none of the abundant fruits of the region has the legendary appeal of the durian, which is difficult to grow, perilous to harvest, and expensive to buy. From late spring through much of the summer, depending on the country, its distinctive aroma pervades the markets of Bangkok and Kuala Lumpur, Rangoon and Jakarta, and well-heeled connoisseurs vie for the opportunity to pay as much as US$25 for a single specimen of some particularly prized variety. Even the cheapest kinds—including one the Thais call "Deception" because it looks from the outside as if it contains large quantities of meat but doesn't—can make a sizeable dent in the budget of a poor family, but it is an expense they will gladly bear two or three times during the season for a sample of its haunting flavor. Devotees further afield must be willing to pay far more: a recent visitor to Tokyo spotted a beautifully boxed durian in a gourmet food shop selling for US$150.

Nobody knows for sure exactly where the durian originated, but it was almost certainly in Malaysia that it was first recognized as a delicacy and the first hybrids were developed. Conceivably, wild animals were responsible for attracting human attention to the fruit, for it seems to have a powerful appeal to them. Elephants generally get the first taste, thanks to their ability to break the spiny shell, followed by rhinoceros, tigers, wild pigs, deer, and monkeys. In Malaysia, there are gruesome tales of people "who have gathered fruits only to be gathered in turn by a hungry elephant".

Both the botanical and the common names come from the Malay *duren*, meaning "thorn" or "prickle". When botanists came to choose a specific descriptive term, they revealed the basic European aversion to the fruit by selecting *zibethinus*, derived from the Italian *zibetto* meaning "civet" or "strong smelling".

Curiously, the earliest Western accounts of the durian fail to mention its odour, perhaps because they were not based on direct experience. Thus the first recorded description, by an Italian traveller of the fifteenth century named Nicolo Conti, says that in Sumatra "they have a green fruit . . . big as a watermelon. Inside are five things like elongated oranges, and resembling thick butter, with a combination of flavours". A century later, a Portuguese explorer named Mendoza also reported what he had heard about the durian. It was supposedly so good, he noted, "that I have heard it affirmed by many that have gone about the world that it doth exceed in savour all others that they have ever seen or tasted. Some do say that have seen it that it seemeth to be that wherewith Adam did transgress, being carried away by the singular savor."

Once they actually smelled the fruit, however, few Europeans were tempted to follow Adam's example. The Dutch in Indonesia gave it the unlovely nickname of *stancker*, and the English in their colonies were just as unappreciative. "Carrion in custard" pronounced a Governor-General of the Straits Settlements, while an Englishman in Ceylon, similarly repulsed, called it "French custard passed through a sewer pipe". Many other popular descriptions were unprintable, so that the average foreigner who ventured into a durian-producing country was disinclined even to taste one. If they did, their attitude was often that of a woman traveller named Rachel Wheatcroft, who called the experience "one of the heroic acts of a timorous existence", and, not surprisingly, did not enjoy the result.

There were some notable exceptions to this general disparagement, however, among them the famous naturalist Alfred Russel Wallace, co-founder with Charles Darwin of the theory of evolution. Wallace was introduced to the durian on the island of Borneo in the mid-nineteenth century and at first had the conventional reaction to the odour. But then, he wrote, one day "I found a ripe fruit on the ground and, eating it out of doors, I at once became a confirmed durian eater". Saying that the consistency and flavour were "indescribable", Wallace promptly proceeded to try, though in far more flattering terms than most of his fellow countrymen. "A rich, butter-like custard highly flavoured with almonds gives the best general idea of it," he thought, "but intermingled with it come wafts of flavor that call to mind cream-cheese, onion-sauce, brown sherry, and other incongruities."

Such conflicting opinions are rare among the natives of Southeast Asia, where an army of durian aficionados agree wholeheartedly with Wallace's final conclusion: "The more you eat of it the less you feel inclined to stop." One ancient Burmese king, for example, is supposed to have become so enamoured of the durians grown in a certain small village he passed through on a royal tour that he struck an unusual bargain with the inhabitants: instead of paying their annual tribute to the throne in gold and precious stones, they could bring him a selection of their prized fruit. Yet another king of that country, distressed to find that durians would not grow well near his capital of Ava, organized a regular system of relay riders to bring a supply in from orchards near the coast during the season.

The most popular way of eating durian, of course, is fresh and at the peak of ripeness, a stage that knowing customers can determine by the colour of the shell and by brushing the fingernails lightly over the spines and listening to the reverberations. Thai durian sellers claim that by the latter method they can tell you the exact day when the fruit will be ready; some even go so far as to specify whether it should be opened in the morning or afternoon.

Durian lovers are loth to do without the taste for more than half the year, however, so a number of methods of preservation have been devised. The Malays, for example, pickle it in salt for use as a relish, while the Thais turn it into a sticky, sweet confection that can be eaten like candy or used to flavour ice cream. A synthetic durian flavour has even been produced, though true devotees deny that any chemical combination can accurately approach the ambrosia of the real thing.

The uses of the durian do not stop with the pleasure of eating it. For centuries it has been regarded as a powerful aphrodisiac, and while modern medical science refuses to lend support to such a contention the old belief still stubbornly persists. More prosaically, the fruit and different parts of the tree have a variety of medicinal and household uses. Malaysians boil the roots to make a concoction to relieve fever, and water in which the leaves have been simmered is held as effective for bathing victims of jaundice. Thais think durian eaten in quantity is good at expelling internal parasites; they also apply the leaves to boils and eat the ground shell to ease heartburn. Dried, the shell makes a useful fuel in many places and when still fresh and aromatic it is placed under sleeping areas in some parts of Thailand to discourage bed bugs.

Thanks to the durian's sharp, hard spines, it has also acquired another more sinister use. During the Pacific War the Japanese sometimes employed the fruit as an instrument of torture, dropping it from a height on the faces of hapless victims; and in Thailand, because of the frequency with which combatants have seized upon a handy durian to settle a dispute, it has gained the distinction of being perhaps the only fruit in the world officially classified as a weapon. "Wielding a durian with intention to strike" is a punishable offense, and the resulting fine is based on the number of puncture marks inflicted.

The principal reason durians cost so much is the finicky growing habits of the tree, especially of the more prized varieties. To begin with, these do well only in soil that has a high sulphur content and no salt; should even a small amount of salt water enter the orchards for any reason—as sometimes happens in Thailand during major floods—the fruit will drop before ripening, thus sending the market price spiralling and driving addicts to despair.

Another peculiarity is that the longer it takes a tree to bear fruit, the better the quality. In Thailand, for instance, the cheapest, least meaty durians like "Deception" can be harvested in only three years, whereas the much esteemed "Golden Pillow", by far the most expensive, does not appear for eight to ten years. Just to compound the difficulty, the quantity of fruit on a tree is in inverse ratio to its quality, the commonplace ones bearing between fifty and eighty and the better ones thirty or less.

Even when all possible care is taken over soil, site, and tree selection, however, durian growing is still enshrouded by a certain degree of mystery; and for reasons nobody can pin down precisely, some localities are simply better than others. Malaysian villages so favoured often advertise the fact by putting the name of the fruit in front of their own, as in the case of Durian Sabatang in Perak and Durian Tawar in Pahang, thus ensuring a steady stream of customers during the season.

Many assert the best durians in all of Asia are grown in Thailand, and of these the most valued varieties traditionally came from orchards on the right bank of the Chao Phraya River in Bangkok, the area where I got my first taste. To some extent this has changed today, with the development of a number of new growing areas less susceptible to floods; even so, fruit from this district is still called "inside" durian to distinguish it from that produced elsewhere, known as "outside". Given a choice, no older Thai would pick an "outside" durian over an "inside" specimen, even when the two are of the same variety. This led in the past to some sharp competitive practices on the part of "outside" growers eager to cash in on the lucrative trade. Back in the sixties, for example, there was a scandal when they started slipping their products into "inside" markets, often by night, in the hope of deluding unwary customers; a special police squad had to be formed to stop the smuggling and save the reputation of "inside" orchards.

A few years after my introduction, I decided to revisit some of the orchards in the company of a knowledgeable Thai friend who claims to have eaten all of the dozens of varieties grown in his country. We started out from the Oriental Hotel, and as we moved up the busy Chao Phraya in a long-tail motorboat he gave me a short introductory course in Thai durian nomenclature.

"If you ask for 'Golden Pillow'," he said, "everyone will know you're a real connoisseur because that's the king of durians. It's got the most meat, the most delicate flavour. They'll also know you're rich because it's the most expensive. The first 'Golden Pillows' didn't appear on the market until about thirty years ago, and they're still relatively scarce. Most well-to-do Thais have to settle for 'Long Stem' which is almost as good but not quite."

Some popular varieties, I learned, have imaginative names, given for reasons that might not be readily apparent to a foreigner. "Gibbon", for instance, is so called because the shell has a brownish tint that supposedly resembles the colour of that animal's fur. "Frog" acquired its name because admirers thought its dark-yellow flesh resembled that of a freshly-skinned amphibian; though no one seems to know the derivations of some of its sub-species like "The Old Woman's Frog", "The Old Man's Frog", and "The Frog on the Bank". One of the cheapest durians is "Golden Button", the meat of which is so thin that the colour of the seed shows through it.

"Then there's 'Transvestite,'" my friend said as our boat turned off the river into a narrow, shady *klong*. "That gets its name because two fruits often appear on the same stem and because it usually won't germinate." Seeing my expression, he quickly added, "It also happens to be one of the best varieties. Excellent flavour."

Our boat moored near an orchard of lofty durian trees, and as we walked along a path that led to the owner's house I saw the fruit hanging like huge, dangerous Christmas ornaments among the dark, glossy leaves. Harvesting can be a hazardous operation, my friend remarked, since the spiny delicacies tend to fall soon after they become ripe.

"Some of the trees get up to sixty feet tall," he said, "and if a durian hits you from that height you'd better be wearing a helmet. Or it may just break open on the ground and then there's nothing to do but eat it fast. Usually the growers pick the fruit three or four days before they ripen, but that takes a lot of knowledge, too. It you pick it too soon, the flavour is never quite as good."

The owner of the orchard was a woman with a dark, weather-beaten face and a broad, welcoming smile. She seemed a little surprised to find a *farang* interested in her pungent produce, but when my friend explained that I was a true durian lover she nodded with approval. We joined a group of five or six people at a long table on which were piled about a dozen durians of assorted sizes and shapes. A large, sharp knife lay nearby.

"This orchard grows several different varieties, " my friend said. "It's well known for the quality of its fruit and these people have come to buy the first of the season."

The atmosphere was as solemn and as anticipatory as the tasting ritual of a great French vineyard. When she perceived that everyone was ready, the owner selected a specimen and deftly sliced it open with the knife. Though the fruit was a relatively small one, I was surprised by the amount of creamy pulp revealed—far more than many of the much larger durians I had eaten in the past. My friend nodded approvingly.

"Frog," the woman said, handing each of us a segment, which we proceeded to eat with our hands. A murmur of appreciation went around the table.

"Excellent flavour," my friend pronounced. "She's famous for her Frogs."

We then sampled two different kinds of Frog, a Long Stem of exceptional delicacy, and a Transvestite that was every bit as good as my friend had promised. After we finished there was a friendly debate over the relative merits of the durians we had sampled, with the first Frog finally winning a majority of votes as the best. Each of us ended up buying one from the proud orchard owner before we left.

As we moved down the shady *klong*, surrounded by the prevalent smell that was now so familiar to me, I mentioned to my friend a comment made by Sir Henry Yule, an English traveller who went on a mission to the Burmese court of Ava in 1855. Durian, said Yule, was "the prince of fruits to those who like it but the chief of abominations to all strangers and novices".

He laughed. "Thank goodness there are so many strangers and novices," he said. "Otherwise there wouldn't be enough durians to go around."

12

THE LOTUS

"How untarnished as it rises from its bed of mud! How modestly it bathes in the clear pond! It is unobstructed within and straight without; it does not spread unrestrained and does not branch out. Its fragrance is more unalloyed the farther it is away; it stands upright gracefully. It is good to behold from a distance but it tolerates no intimacy."

At one time every Chinese school child could recite this passage from the eleventh-century Confucian scholar Chou Tun-yi, memorized as part of their instruction on what constituted a "perfect man". Moreover, they were regularly reminded of it by the living presence of Chou's ostensible subject, for all around them the delicate pink or white lotus did indeed emerge undefiled from the muddy bottoms of lakes and ponds, temple pools and large water jars on terraces. It was an integral part of their landscape, as it was of their culture.

Throughout much of Asia, *Nelumbium speciosum*—from *nelumbo*, the Sinhalese name—has played a similarly prominent role, probably bearing more symbolic weight than any other plant in the world. In one culture or another, over some 5,000 years, the lotus has represented creation, the various stages of life, purity, female beauty, resilience, peace, prosperity, perfection, fruitfulness, summer, resurrection, dreaminess, truth, harmony, and the sun, to mention only some. It has been employed as a motif on porcelains, palaces, and pagodas, has inspired countless poems, and has figured prominently in several major religious and philosophical concepts. At the same time, on a more practical level, it has turned up on the dinner table in a wide variety of preparations ranging from the humble to the highly exotic.

Considering its complex cultural history, it is perhaps not surprising that the lotus has also provoked a certain amount of misunderstanding. Any student of Western literature is familiar with Lord Alfred Tennyson's "mild-eyed, melancholy lotos-eaters", just as he is with Homer's account in the *Odyssey* of a similarly-named tribe whose addiction to the plant caused them to live in a state of permanent forgetfulness.

Naturally this has led some to assume that the fabled Asian lotus and the amnesia-producing plant of Greek legend were one and the same. The author of a novel about Thailand, for instance, wrote evocatively of "adventurous men who succumbed to the bright eyes of brown maidens who fed them lotus fruits picked fresh from green, cone-shaped seed cases".

Actually Homer was referring to another plant entirely, a prickly shrub called *Ziziphus lotus*, which grows in Greece and parts of North Africa and produces a honey-sweet fruit; the latter was used to make a strong fermented drink popularly believed to induce a state of dreamy contentment.

Ancient Egyptians were the first to employ "lotus bud" capitals at the top of building columns, and many books refer to the importance of the plant from the earliest Pharaonic times. Horus, the Sun God, is supposed to have been born from a lotus, the flower was often placed on royal mummies, and it was the emblem of Upper Egypt.

Again, though, these common beliefs are botanically incorrect. The plant so celebrated was, in fact, a variety of *Nymphaea*, or water lily, a quite different species which grew freely along the Nile and was much admired for its blue flowers. The true lotus came to the region considerably later, probably around the fifth century B.C., when the

Persians invaded Egypt. It obviously became well established, however, for Herodotus (b. 484 B.C.) was certainly referring to *Nelumbium* when he wrote, "There are other lilies, like roses, that grow in the river, the fruit of which is contained in a separate pod that springs up from the root, in form very like a wasp's nest. In this there are many berries fit to be eaten, of the size of an olive-stone, and they are eaten both fresh and dried."

Nelumbium itself is indigenous all across central Asia from India to China and Japan. The leaves grow out of long, creeping rootstocks and, unlike those of the water lily, rise some distance above the surface of the water. One of their peculiar features is that they quickly shed any water that falls on them, not because they are waxy, as many suppose, but owing to a network of closely-set minute hairs that cover them.

The flowers, standing above the leaves, are large and usually white or pink, though striped and rose-colored, as well as double-flowering varieties have been cultivated. Special hybrids include the "Double-necked lotus", on which one flower supersedes another, and the "Double-headed lotus", which has two flowers on a single stalk.

Seeds of the plant, each in a separate hole, appear in a flat-topped receptacle that does indeed resemble a wasp's nest. Tests have shown them to have an exceptionally long viability; of three 2,000-year-old lotus seeds found in a peat bog near Tokyo in 1951, two germinated, flowered, and produced seeds of their own, which in turn were distributed to botanical gardens around the world.

The only non-Asian lotus is a yellow-flowering species called *Nelumbium luteum*, native to North America and commonly called the Duck Acorn.

Many Westerners tend to associate the lotus almost exclusively with Buddhism because of the important role it has played in the symbolism of that religion for almost two millennia. If fact, though, it had achieved legendary prominence long before the Buddha's doctrines spread throughout Asia. The early Aryans of India called it the Dawn Lily and associated it with the birth of the day. A figure of a goddess unearthed in the Indus valley and dating from 3,000 B.C. wears a lotus in her hair and nothing else; later female divinities like Padma, Kali, and Lakai were also nearly always shown with the flower, either sitting or standing on it or holding one in their hands. In Brahman mythology, the creator was said to have sprung from a lotus which grew out of Visnu's navel as he lay in meditation. An ancient Sanskrit poet wrote of his beloved, "Thy eyes are two lotus buds, thy hand the full-blown flower, thy arms its graceful roots"; and beautiful women have been similarly compared ever since wherever the lotus grows.

To Koreans, it was the Daughter of the Sun, or the Flower that Speaks. Japanese, on the other hand, particularly associated the plant with death and the spirit world; little lotus flowers made of gold or silver paper are still carried at funerals, and food offerings to ancestral spirits are often wrapped in the leaves. In one of the classic Japanese flower arrangements past, present, and future are represented by a partly-decayed leaf and seed-pod, a newly opened leaf and flower, and a closed leaf and bud.

But it was in China, perhaps, that the lotus was most firmly established as part of the culture and daily life of the people. Since the very earliest times, ideographs were devised for every part of the plant, from the root to the fruiting receptacle and seed, and most of them also acquired double meanings and connotations that were useful to Chinese writers.

For example, when the poet Huang T'ing-chien wrote "The seeds in their pod remind me/Of brothers under the same roof", he could be sure that his readers made the connection between *lien-tzu*, "lotus-seed", and its connotative suggestion of "successive (births of) sons". Similarly, since the character for "lotus root" can also be a pun meaning "a pair of lovers", Hsu Chao was able to achieve added poignancy in this brief, haunting little poem:

> Since you went away
> Dust has collected on the lute;
> The seeds have grown into lotuses—
> When will there be a lotus-root?

Ho Hsien Ku, one of the Taoist Eight Immortals, holds a lotus in his hand, and in some parts of China incense was burned to the Spirit of the Lotus to ward off misfortune. As the emblem of summer, it was widely used as a decorative motif on everything from carpets to opera costumes, rivalled only by the peony in popularity among floral possibilities.

One of the strangest associations came in the practice of binding women's feet. According to legend this began near the end of the T'ang Dynasty with Li Yu, a prince and poet who ruled over southern China from 961 to 975. His favourite concubine, called Precious Beauty, was famed for her slim figure and talent for dancing. One day the prince gave her a huge golden lotus, six feet high and decorated with pearls; then he asked her to bind her feet with silk so that they were like crescent moons and made her dance within the calyx of the flower. Within a short time foot-binding became the rage among dancers attached to the Imperial Palace and the fashion spread throughout the nobility. In the 11th century the poet Su Tung-p'o wrote "She dances in a perfumed cloud with tiny lotus feet/Sad sometimes, but gracious and light/She dances like the wind and leaves no trace. . ."

The term "Golden Lotus" was awarded the smallest foot, measuring three inches at the most. A four-inch specimen was a "Silver Lotus", while an "Iron Lotus" was so large it was scarcely worth mentioning. A whole category of erotic literature, as well as pornographic paintings, grew out of the supposed charms of such deformed feet and their effect on besotted men, ending only when the practice declined at the beginning of the present century.

Vast ponds of lotus were a common sight all over China, and their annual blooming was looked upon as a good omen for the coming harvest. Lotus-viewing was also regarded as one of the great aesthetic experiences of the year, especially in the ponds and moats of Beijing. Within the walls of the Forbidden City, three enormous artificial lakes were filled with the plants, the leaves of which rose as high as seven feet above the water, topped by the spectacular flowers. An intricate network of waterways was cleared so that small punts could wind their way beneath the fragrant canopy.

But visual delight was not the only reason for cultivating the lotus. It was also—and still is—grown extensively as a commercial crop, particularly along the Yangtze River valley, since every part of the plant is put to some practical use as food or otherwise.

The thick, strong tubers can be eaten raw or cooked, and an easily digestible starch made from them is often given to old or sick people for nourishment. They also yield long, silky fibres, not strong enough to be woven into textiles—though one of the Immortals is described as wearing clothes made of lotus silk—but useful as lamp wicks. The leaves, fresh or dried, are used to wrap food in markets and also impart a delicate flavour to meats which are covered with them and steamed. The seeds, rich in protein and carbohydrates, are boiled in sugar or eaten raw when young; dried, they can be ground into flour or used in medicines.

In *Six Characters of a Floating Life*, we are told that Yun, wife of Shen Fu, made gauze tea-leaf bags which she then tucked inside open lotus blossoms. When the petals closed in the evening, the bags were trapped inside and by morning would be scented with the fragrance.

Even more esoteric uses have been found for the flowers. The yellow stamens, when dried, are employed as a cosmetic, and the pollen is regarded by some as an effective ingredient in love potions. Preparations made from the white lotus are said to rejuvenate the faces of old people, while dried petals of flowers given as offerings are the basis of a tea drunk by pregnant women for a less painful labour.

The Chinese also used lotus seeds to test the density of brine. If four or five out of ten heavier seeds floated in the water, it was considered to be strong; however, if all the seeds sank the water was useless for the purposes of salt extraction.

The lotus was thus well established in most of the leading Asian cultures by the time Buddhism adopted it as a major symbol. This appears to have been done at the very beginning; in the oldest Buddhist art, the lotus is one of the four basic emblems used to represent the Buddha's life, the others being the bodhi tree, the wheel of law, and the pagoda, and it can be seen as such on coins, votive tablets, and temple decorations. When the Master began to be depicted in human form, around the first century A.D., he was nearly always shown sitting or standing on an open lotus flower. In imitation of the former, Buddhist priests often assume what is called the "lotus position", regarded as particularly useful in producing the physical and mental calm needed for deep meditation.

Like so many others before them, Buddhists found the lotus to be rich in symbolic possibilities. The wheel-like shape of the five flower petals was thought to typify the doctrine of endless cycles of existence, just as the appearance of the seed pods, blossom, and bud at the same time was a convenient representation of past, present, and future. They, too, were struck by the pristine beauty of the lotus as it grew from the mud and read into this the power of the soul to rise out of murky evil into the light of a better existence.

The tendency of water to gather on the leaves in shimmering, jewel-like drops was also seen as significant. In remote Tibet, out of the lotus' natural growing range, it inspired the famous mystic incantantation *Om mani padme hum*, which means: "May my soul be like the gem-like dew drop which lies on the lip of the lotus leaf before it falls into the peaceful obscurity of the lake."

The Chinese added these Buddhist views of the lotus to their own already lengthy list and supplied some others. One, widely depicted in painting, was their concept of the Western Heaven and its Sacred Lotus Lake, the latter often reproduced in temple courtyards. According to this belief, each soul on earth has its own lotus in the lake, waiting for the proper time to bloom. The plants of the wicked fail to thrive and the buds droop sadly, while those of the very devout open splendidly as soon as the person dies, allowing his soul to ascend straight to heaven. The divinity Amitabha is usually shown enthroned above this sea of blossoms and lovely pavilions float about in the sky.

(The Lotus Lake has found its way from China to other Asian cultures, though not always with Amitabha in attendance. A nineteenth-century painter in Thailand named Khrua In Khong adorned the walls of a Bangkok temple with a haunting series of almost surrealistic Westernized murals, one of which shows a gigantic lotus rising from a lake of lesser blooms. This has been mistakenly identified by some as a fanciful depiction of the annual Loy Krathong ceremony, when little banana-leaf vessels in the shape of lotus flowers are set adrift in rivers and canals as offerings to the water spirits. But the lotuses in Khrua In Khong's lake are clearly not boats, and to anyone familiar with the legend of the Western Heaven the symbolism of the great central bloom is obvious.)

"The fairest flower of the East", as one writer has called it, the lotus remains as ubiquitous as ever, "auspicious when worn, health-giving when eaten, a synonym for beauty in many languages". From India to China, countless thousands of Buddha images sit serenely on its stylized petals, looking down on altars adorned with the real flower—sometimes freshly opened as in Sri Lanka or deftly folded buds as in Thailand. The Hindu goddess Kali still displays a lotus to symbolize eternal generation, and the Taoist Ho Hsien Ku holds one to represent open-heartedness. The classic simplicity of its form continues to inspire artists in almost every medium. Moreover, both farmers and epicures go on benefiting from its vast range of culinary possibilities.

In Chinese the lotus is called *lien* or *ho*. The former, though written differently, sounds like the word for "unite" and the latter suggests "harmony". This seems fitting, for certainly no other flowering plant can rival it in uniting the cultures of Asia so harmoniously.

13

THE MYTH OF ASIAN WOMEN

O f all the popular myths associated with what was once called the mysterious East, none has proved so haunting, or so durable, as the Western image of the Asian woman. Just when she began to exert her powerful allure it would be difficult to say; conceivably she was part of Marco Polo's exotic baggage, along with other wonders from the court of the great Khan. Whenever it was, she clearly filled an urgent need and long ago established herself as a permanent fixture in the wistful fancies of countless Walter Mittys of the West.

She wears a variety of costumes—the sari and the sarong, the kimono and the ao-dai—but her mythical nature is remarkably consistent from culture to culture, and will be at once familiar to any movie-goer or reader of romantic novels.

She is beautiful—that goes almost without saying: eyes almond-shaped and usually downcast, hair like a jet waterfall, skin cool and flawless and scented with some subtle fragrance. Her voice is soft, never rising in anger and little more than a musical moan in the throes of passion. The latter sound is not uncommon, for she is, of course, sublimely sensual: that modesty, that child-like charm, that grace that can turn a chopstick into a magic wand, all conceal a sexual appetite of tigerish voraciousness, adept in techniques yet unexplored even in our current literature.

Above all, she is subservient; and here, I suspect, we approach the real source of the myth's potent appeal. Beauty, after all, is a matter of taste, and sensuality isn't uniquely Asian, however artfully employed. Utter submissiveness, though, is something very special. It is all very well for Caitlin Thomas, widow of Dylan, to write that a woman's proper place is "in bed or at the sink, and the extent of her travels should be from one to the other and back"; but the hard truth is that few of her Western sisters agree with her, even in Wales. The mythical Asian woman, on the other hand, not only knows her place but wouldn't dream of changing it. She positively dotes on serving her master, scrubbing his back in his bath, performing quaint little dances for his amusement, even providing him with others of her kind should his interest wane.

Thus the myth, and a charming one it is to many males reeling under the impact of the feminist revolution, beleaguered in their strongholds of chauvinism. Unfortunately, though, things are not what they seem. Prospective emigrants all ready to give up their citizenships and pass through the pearly gates should be apprised that, at heart, the myth has about as much validity as the belief that chop suey is an old Chinese speciality.

My own first pinprick of doubt came long ago, when I was thinking about renting a house in Bangkok and went to call on the owner. He was a prominent businessman and he, his wife, and I sat on his spacious veranda discussing the house in question. Or rather he and I discussed it; the wife, for the most part, sat quietly by, flashing the celebrated Thai smile now and again but taking little part in the conversation. This did not surprise me; in those innocent early days I assumed that as a typical Asian woman she had little interest in her husband's business affairs and was only present to make sure we had an ample supply of iced jasmine tea.

I realized my mistake when we reached the question of money. The husband named a sum that was reasonable and, still better, several hundred baht lower that the housing allowance I was given by the university where I worked. The wife promptly murmured something in Thai and the husband, with a sheepish smile, said he had made a mistake. The rent was slightly higher: exactly the amount of my allowance, as a matter of fact. As I was leaving, he accompanied me to the gate and said, "Actually if you want to discuss it more you might as well see my wife. She handles all the house rentals."

After a few other similar experiences, I began to look a little more closely into the ancestry of the Asian woman. I had read some history and knew that it provided considerable evidence that, on the surface at least, appeared strongly to support the myth. Both Confucian and Buddhist doctrines, I knew, held women in very low esteem, the latter going so far as to assert they might as well give up the idea of attaining Nirvana without first passing through reincarnation as a man.

In tenth-century Heian Japan, they were barred from taking any part in public affairs, and women of the higher class passed most of their time in semi-darkness, behind screens. Well-born Chinese girls had their feet bound from birth, producing deformed little stumps that presumably kept them from straying far afield. In Hindu countries they disappeared into purdah after marriage, and if they were unlucky enough to be widowed they were expected to join their husbands on the funeral pyre. The old Siamese liked to say that "a woman is the hind legs of the elephant" (it was naturally unnecessary to identify the forelegs), and a man was allowed to have as many wives as he could afford.

All this I knew, but as I went through the history books again, I found a remarkable number of exceptions—so many that I began to wonder how things really operated down among the unrecorded masses. Our vivid knowledge of Heian Japan, for example, comes from none of those supposedly dominant men but from the writings of two women, Murasaki Shikibu (*The Tale of Genji*) and Sei Shonagon (*The Pillow Book*), neither of whom sounds exactly downtrodden. Chinese women might have been hobbled, but one of them rose from a third-grade concubine to the throne of the Manchu dynasty as the Dowager Empress Tzu Hsi. Some measure of *her* gentle ways might be taken from the following edict which she handed down after a treason trial: "As to Su Shun [one of the defendants], his treasonable guilt far exceeds that of his accomplices and he fully deserves the punishment of dismemberment and the slicing process. But we cannot make up our mind to impose this extreme penalty and therefore, in our clemency, we sentence him to immediate decapitation."

In Vietnam, I discovered the Trung sisters, who led the first uprising against the Chinese in 39 A.D. and proclaimed themselves jointly as queen. When they were overthrown, they committed joint suicide by jumping into a river together. And in Thailand, I found a sixteenth-century queen who was certainly not content to be the hind legs of an elephant: she mounted one of the animals during a war with Burma and helped win a crucial battle, losing her life in the process but earning a prominent niche in Thai history.

Getting up into more contemporary times, I found an equally rich assortment of ladies who hardly conformed to the stereotype. I doubt that any American senator who ever dealt with Madame Chiang Kai Shek emerged still regarding Chinese women as pitiable beasts of burden out of Pearl Buck. If so, he had only to contemplate little Chiang Ching in the halcyon days of her bloody Cultural Revolution not too many years ago.

Madame Sirimavo Bandaranaike of Sri Lanka often shed tears during her political speeches, but that didn't prevent her becoming the world's first woman prime minister or from nationalizing the foreign businesses on her picturesque island. In nearby India, politicians quickly discovered how unwise it was to cross *their* lady prime minister, Indira Gandhi. And one must not forget Vietnam's Madame Nhu, with her enthusiasm for priestly barbecues, nor overlook the lovely Imelda Marcos, whom her husband once referred to as his "secret weapon" because of her vote-getting skills (more recently her prowess for staying out of jail).

Fiction tends to be a less fertile field for research into the true Asian woman, since novelists naturally have more to gain by keeping the myth intact. Most Oriental heroines are variations on either the forsaken Cio-Cio-San of "Madame Butterfly", fluttering helplessly in the shadow of Fuji, or Miss Buck's O-Lan, planting rice, bearing children, and just plain enduring. Now and then, though, one catches disturbing glimpses.

There is, for instance, the White Leopard, the bar-girl in Jack Reynolds' *A Woman of Bangkok*, who contemplates her customers in this passage: "By and large she preferred Americans to all the rest. The English were too sentimental: they always fell a little bit in love with even a dancing-girl, even though they were going to be in town only one night and never see her again . . . . As for the Dutch, they were always fat and quarrelsome about money. The French paid too little and never gave a girl any peace all night and also they always wanted to do things that the Buddha doesn't approve of. But the Americans knew how to treat a girl like her. They had plenty of money and were free with it when out to enjoy themselves."

And there is a scene in Graham Greene's *The Quiet American* in which Fowler, the English narrator, worries aloud to his Vietnamese mistress about his inability to match the various forms of security being offered her by his American rival. "There are always ways," she says thoughtfully. "You could take out life insurance."

And what about ordinary Asian women, the ones who don't make the history books? I'm afraid my notebooks are full of depressing discoveries. Ponder, for instance, the results of a poll taken some years ago in Tokyo. More than half the younger Japanese husbands interviewed confessed that they "feared" their wives. Back-scrubbing may still take the edge off a hard day in some households, but four out of five husbands said they turn their entire paycheck over to the shy young thing that wields the brush and three-fourths said they would-n't think of staying out after ten at night without checking first to make sure it was all right. A staggering eighty-five percent admitted that they were forced to shine their own shoes.

In Thailand prosperous men often have a whole bevy of mistress-es—"minor wives" as they are charmingly called—but this situation is scarcely the sensual delight it may seem to an outsider. The various ladies may well tolerate one another—they often do—but only at a price, which generally means separate but equal establishments for each, plus fringe benefits for a horde of relatives. Apart from multi-plying domestic problems to an incredibly complex degree (some polygamous husbands spend almost all their time sorting out family squabbles involving the distribution of their wealth), this can obvious-ly be very expensive; when one powerful military leader died in the early 1960s, it was found that he had helped himself to over ten mil-lion dollars from the national treasury and that most of it had gone to his forty-odd minor wives.

A man I once knew in Ayutthaya, the old capital, had two wives who shared his house. It was an interesting establishment sociologi-cally because the two happened to be twin sisters and because they always managed to get pregnant simultaneously—once they delivered on the same day. But it was no paradise for the husband. They ganged up on him, he used to tell me, and he always lost. To make matters worse, they moved their mother in, which meant he had three oppo-nents in every argument. They took over his shop and often locked him out of the house at night to show their displeasure. To escape the whole sorry mess, he finally went into the priesthood, where I believe he remains to this day.

Three out of four divorce actions in Japan are initiated now by women. Divorce is still relatively rare in Thailand, but ageing "number one wives" do not, like old soldiers, simply fade away. To compensate them for the loss of his full-time company (and also to keep them quiet), the husband usually gives them a few title deeds and perhaps a business or two to occupy their idle hours. Which may explain why today women own or control the majority of Bangkok's choicest real estate, as well as a large number of its shops, too.

When the latter is the case, they are noted for their ability to drive a hard bargain, however demure they may look. Not long ago, talking to a friend, I mentioned an antique shop I liked because of its friendly proprietor and reasonable prices. He shook his head sadly: "Don't go there now. The wife's behind the counter." Nothing more needed to be said.

The truth is that one of the real Asian woman's most notable characteristics is her immense practicality, unblemished by such weaknesses as sentimentality and a trusting nature. Long ago she learned (or was perhaps born with the knowledge) that title deeds, a gold necklace, and a few savings accounts scattered about here and there are far more comforting than any of the abstractions men seem to prize; and a major part of her energy and thought is directed toward acquiring as many of these useful things as possible. Scratch a geisha, or a "minor wife", or a matronly Hong Kong housewife, and you will find the soul of a gifted and single-minded cost accountant. In all probability what Cio-Cio-San was really thinking about as she gazed forlornly over Nagasaki harbour was how her lover's desertion would affect her bank balance.

Finally, most devastating of all, she really doesn't feel in the least inferior to men. Laws and tradition might proclaim her so, but she, in her infinite wisdom, knows better. Madame Bandaranaike put it rather bluntly when she commented that "Men politicians are all weak". An old Thai saying expresses the view more delicately but also, perhaps, even more witheringly: "A good wife is like a mother to her husband."

14

A LAOTIAN INTERLUDE

(The following piece, in slightly different form, was written in the winter of 1969, and Laos today, of course, is a very different place. I have included it mostly for its nostalgic interest but also because it suggests that some aspects never change.)

If the recent Congressional subcommittee looking into United States involvement in Laos had paid a visit to its capital city in the guise of ordinary tourists, its members might well have come away with at least two unexpected impressions. First of all, after a few days in Vientiane—which a British diplomat once described as "a rather sordid Garden of Eden"—they might well have concluded that, far from being at war, Laos isn't even in a state of particular unrest. Second, they might have decided that not only is there no widespread American involvement, there are practically no Americans here at all.

A closer inspection would alter both conclusions, but the fact remains that at first, or even second, sight, Vientiane hardly seems a city where the enemy is quite literally at the gates—a unit of Pathet Lao soldiers passed the night within two kilometres of the city limits not long ago. Their side controls the entire eastern half of the country, which includes the areas bordering on North and South Vietnam. The government forces control the main towns and villages to the west, and the Mekong River Valley.

The seat of Prince Souvanna Phouma's government, Vientiane is the administrative capital of the country, as distinct from the royal capital at Luang Prabang; and from news dispatches on its strategic and political importance, one could easily imagine it as a teeming national centre of the order of Bangkok, or at any rate, Kuala Lumpur. In fact, it is the smallest capital in Asia—about 180,000 is the population figure usually given, but no census has ever been taken, either of the city or of the country—and by all odds the most somnolent. Residents claim it is now undergoing a boom period, which to judge from past accounts may well be true; but in Laos booms, like most other things, tend to be muted, and it is hard to see Vientiane's in quite the same light as those being enjoyed (or suffered) by certain cities across the Mekong River in Thailand.

Apart from the peculiarities of Laotian temperament, one reason for this is undoubtedly the absence of the obvious American influence so evident in Thai centres of U.S. military activity like Khorat, Ubol, and Udorn Thani, all of which are relatively close to Laos on the other side of the river. In those places, the influence is all-pervasive, and for anyone who knew them in the old days it has rendered them almost unrecognizable. The streets are bustling with American traffic and lined with bars, pizza shops, and massage parlours bearing American names, and the Americans themselves, both servicemen and dependents, are very much in evidence everywhere.

Vientiane, on the other hand, for all its importance in the politics of Southeast Asia, has remained substantially what it was before any newspaper editor ever heard of it: a leisurely, slightly rundown French colonial town built on the site of an ancient capital to administer a remote country that had (and has) few roads, no railways, and a population described fondly by one observer as "the least urgent souls on earth".

An American who came here in the mid-fifties, as part of what might be called the advance guard, summed up the atmosphere of the capital as "tranquillity just this side of Rip Van Winkle", and claimed its principal activities to be "picknicking on Sunday, watching the sun set over the Mekong, and playing badminton in the front yard". The pace has undeniably picked up since, but it is still a long way from being hectic, and the dominant mood is still a gentle mixture of French decadence and Laotian disdain for unseemly displays of activity.

Some of the decadence is distinctly odd. A favourite activity among certain members of the French community, for example, is driving out to the city abattoir on nights when the moon is full. To avoid offending Buddhist sensibilities, slaughtering of pigs is done after dark in a somewhat remote area; the workers are Chinese and they go about their task by torchlight, almost naked. The spectators supposedly find the combination of nudity, blood, and flickering flames immensely arousing.

Then there was the British diplomat who invited a friend and me to dinner at his colonial-style villa on the edge of town. Dozens of candles provided the sole illumination for the vast open living room, and the staff, composed entirely of handsome young Laotian boys, were dressed in sky-blue silk livery. At one point, when our host went off to do something in the kitchen, my friend looked over my shoulder in considerable alarm; turning, I saw two deer casually stroll into the room, munch delicately from a plate of hors d'oeuvres, and then pass through another door into the garden. Our host laughed when we remarked on this. "Oh, they've become very bold lately. Usually they won't come in when strangers are here. They always eat with me, though, when I'm alone, the boys spoil them so."

The cuisine in the better restaurant is, or aims at being, French, and if the menus include curiosities like hamburgers, the offer is made very discreetly, near the end. There are numerous *patisseries* selling delicious French bread, but only one or two small places brazen enough even to attempt a pizza. At night, the prostitutes on the promenade along the Mekong embankment murmur not "Hey, Joe", but

"Monsieur, un moment s'il vous plaît". If there is a Coca-Cola sign in the entire downtown area, it is remarkably well concealed.

As in every other part of Asia today, Japanese automobiles predominate, but if it isn't a Datsun or a Toyota weaving in and out of the pedicabs on the Rue Samsenthai, it's more likely to be a Citroen than a Ford. In the bar of the Hotel Lan Xang, Vientiane's largest, one encounters a considerable variety of nationalities, ranging from Czech to Indian, but very rarely an American outside a few embassy types and an occasional tourist straying from Thailand.

What makes all this somewhat extraordinary is that there are, by official count (which most people here regard as very conservative), slightly more than 2,000 Americans, including dependents, in Laos and most of them are in Vientiane. The majority of these are supposedly working for the United States Agency for International Development (USAID), an organization that in Laos includes military as well as other kinds of aid, though many of them undoubtedly have duties not covered in official job descriptions. *Open* military assistance by outsiders was prohibited by the Geneva Accords of 1962, which permitted only the French military mission to remain, but neither the government nor the Pathet Lao has ever taken this very seriously.

The American Embassy in Vientiane, which has by far the largest staff of any of the foreign embassies and a telephone book thicker than the one for all of Laos, admits to about seventy "assistant military attachés". In addition, an indeterminate number of the local Americans are either C.I.A. or employees of the agency, which has taken over many of the functions of the former military representatives. The C.I.A. finances—or is generally believed to finance—both Air America (207 Americans officially employed) and Continental Air Charter (73 American employees), on whose planes supplies and personnel are flown to landing strips all over the country.

Though there are no outward signs of the American military presence on the streets of Vientiane itself—not even an occasional army vehicle—there is a good deal of activity at the airport: big-bellied transport planes for dropping supplies upcountry and a large number of helicopters and two-man trainer planes. (There is even more of this sort of thing to be seen at the tranquil little royal capital of Luang Prabang, to which American supply planes frequently fly direct from Thai bases.)

And upcountry there is a sizeable group of other Americans, not included in any embassy count, whose job is the arming, training, and paying of an irregular *"armée clandestine"*, composed mostly of tough, highly individualistic Hmong hill tribesmen who are regarded as more reliable fighters against the Pathet Lao than the regular government forces.

Whether one accepts the official or unofficial figures for the number of Americans at present in Laos, it is still, proportionately, as large as the number stationed in many of those cities that have been so dramatically transformed in Thailand. Moreover, American aid to Laos, in terms of the size of the population, has been greater than that extended to any other Asian country, and normally aid is accompanied not only by personnel but also by culture.

European residents of Vientiane believe three factors probably account for the American non-presence. The first, proudly proclaimed by the French group, is that their own impact—through some fifty-four years of colonial rule and later of strong cultural influence—has been too powerful to dissolve under anything less than the kind of super-American pressure that has been brought to bear on Saigon. Laos was a particular favourite with intellectual French expatriates, who came and went native here with more abandon than in either Cambodia or Vietnam. A large number settled down permanently, many with Laotian wives, and formed the core of the sizeable present-day community; in addition, there are French cultural and information centres, a large French military mission, French-operated schools, and an active embassy that is the unquestioned pacesetter in Vientiane's social life.

The second factor is simply that, however large the controversial American military involvement in Laos may be, most of it is aerial and most of the men concerned are not stationed in Laos at all. They fly their missions from bases in Thailand, and whatever cultural impact they may have is there. In Laos, their impact is in the forms of bombs, which fall on Pathet Lao strongholds in enormous quantities, but out of earshot of Vientiane.

Finally, those Americans who undeniably *are* here live, for the most part, in a world that physically as well as psychologically is singularly isolated from the daily life of the capital. The majority live in one or another of several large housing compounds that have been built for them in the past few years by USAID. The largest of these, a creation that is the object of endless marvel, amusement, and occasional ridicule among other Western residents, is called, with military simplicity, KM-6 because it happens to lie six kilometres from Vientiane.

KM-6 is a remarkably faithful replica of an American suburb, done with the artistry of a Hollywood set. It has straight, clearly marked streets, modern homes with neatly trimmed lawns, a ten-grade American-style school, a softball diamond, a sewage system, and dependable supplies of electricity and water—all of which are novelties in Vientiane. Its families are kept occupied during off-duty hours with activities that include twice-nightly showings of movies, bingo parties, cook-outs, games days, and, of course, the cocktail parties and dinners that are such a feature of suburban life back home. "No wonder they don't come into town," a British resident remarked to me. "They don't have any time."

Even if the Americans were fully integrated into Vientiane's life, though, it's at least debatable whether they would have a very profound effect, for the capital has demonstrated an exceptional aptitude for absorbing all sorts and races of people without disturbing its ambiance. Ever since Laos first attracted the attention of the world, an incredible assortment of foreigners has been flocking to help solve its numerous social, economic, and political problems. Indeed, even before then, non-Laotian, non-French faces were not exactly unfamiliar.

However charmed they were by the carefree atmosphere of the place, the French were forced to conclude that *somebody* had to work *sometime* and the Laotians were plainly disinclined to do so. (According to the English writer Norman Lewis, who travelled extensively through Indochina in the 1950s, "It is considered ill-bred and irreligious in Laos to work more than is necessary," a delightful attitude certainly but not one that eased the burden of colonial administration.)

The sharp, clever, industrious Vietnamese were thus brought in to do what had to be done, such as cooking and collecting taxes, and joining the ubiquitous Chinese and Indians who had traditionally taken care of what commerce there was. Today, these three races still own and operate practically every shop, restaurant, and trading company in Vientiane, a fact that has given them economic control of the city and also earned them a sleepy but palpable resentment from the natives.

But it was in the fifties and early sixties that the really exotic foreigners started coming into the capital. At the Geneva Conference on Indochina in 1954, the world in general became aware for the first time that there was a country called Laos (the "s" was a gift from the French; in the local language it is called Lao) and that it was embroiled in a dangerous little war between the government and Vietminh-backed insurgents who called themselves the Pathet Lao, which means simply "Lao country".

The Pathet Lao won official recognition as a reality at Geneva, as well as control of two provinces on the North Vietnamese border, and soon afterward Laos was plunged into the state of semi-crisis in which it has lived ever since. Governments in Vientiane have come and gone, sometimes peacefully as when the durable Prince Souvanna Phouma resigned in 1958 in the face of objections to his policy of trying to bring the Pathet Lao into the government, sometimes violently as when, in August 1960, an unknown captain in the Second Parachute Battalion named Kong Le staged a revolt against the pro-American government and took control of the capital, only to be driven into the provinces the following December by the U.S.-backed forces of General Phoumi Nosavan.

Yet another Geneva conference was called in 1962, this time with the Laotian problem as the main issue. Fourteen nations attended, including the U.S., Russia, Communist China, Thailand, and North and South Vietnam, all of whom ultimately signed an agreement calling for a coalition government under Souvanna Phouma and the immediate departure of all foreign military personnel with the exception of the French. The idea was to make all of Laos "neutralist", a term that both Kong Le and Souvanna Phouma favored; and though in theory this idea is still in force, in fact it lasted only as long as it took the various delegates to fly home from Geneva and think of less obvious methods of intervention.

While all this was going on, numerous strangers were discovering the charms of Vientiane. There were the consulates and embassies, of course, which increased in both numbers and importance as international interest in Laos grew, and whose ambassadors (particularly those of the big powers like the U.S., Britain, and the U.S.S.R.) dispensed advice to the government with a freedom that may be unique in modern Asian politics. Owing to the suddenness of their interest, there were certain housing problems at first—in 1956 the British embassy was a rather flimsy shack in the middle of a swampy field—but they quickly settled in and established more durable quarters.

There was the International Control Commission, composed of Canadians, Indians, and Poles, who were supposed to supervise the on-and-off truce between the government and the rebel Pathet Lao. There was the United Nations, which sent a stream of representatives from countries as remote as Sweden, Italy, Tunisia, Argentina, and Switzerland to look into Laotian affairs. Other countries less remote, like Thailand, Cambodia, the Philippines, Japan, and both Chinas, also sent people.

Whenever the truce broke down, as it did almost as regularly as Vientiane's electric supply, armies of journalists descended on the city and, from the bar of the Constellation Hotel, tried to write about battles that nobody seemed to know much about. It was a somewhat surrealistic task, reminiscent of Evelyn Waugh's *Scoop*, leading one reporter to announce that when he came to write a book about his experiences, one chapter would be entitled "I was a Pathet Lao Battalion".

As interest in Laos grew, aid of various kinds flowed in, either to influence the outcome of the war or, more humanely, to alter some of the depressing statistics of the country: the poorest communications, the lowest life expectancy, and the lowest literacy rate in all of Southeast Asia. It was to Laos that the late Dr. Tom Dooley came in search of a place to become the American Dr. Albert Schweitzer and, as everybody knows, found it.

Finally, an assortment of dubious world travellers suddenly became aware of the general permissiveness of the place and of the interesting fact that gold and opium were readily available and extraordinarily cheap.

While the Laotian political situation was settling down to a sort of chronic crisis, a good many of these visitors settled down, too, with the result that Vientiane today, whether or not it shows it, must qualify as one of the most cosmopolitan cities in Asia. For example, there are close to a dozen separate aid organizations with their headquarters and staffs, including the Dooley Foundation, the Japanese Overseas Volunteers, the British Voluntary Service Overseas organization, Operation Brotherhood (Filipino), USAID, the Peace Corps, the International Red Cross, the Catholic Relief Services, various agencies of the U.N., and an international Protestant group called World Vision.

In addition, Vientiane has 15 foreign embassies and three consulates, representing, among others, both North and South Vietnam and Communist China. It might be thought that the two Vietnams would raise serious social problems, especially in view of the fact that the North Vietnamese ambassador is at present dean of the diplomatic corps, but according to a reliable source such is not the case. The two are frequently in attendance at the same functions, and if they are not exactly cordial on these occasions, neither are they hostile. "How *could* you be in Vientiane?" asked one veteran partygoer.

The Chinese ambassador offers no social threats at all: he went home for "reorientation" two years ago and hasn't been heard from since. The Chinese embassy, a shuttered, silent place, is run by the chargé d'affaires and, in the opinion of local observers, is kept going mainly as a convenient base from which to direct various clandestine activities in Thailand.

There is also, theoretically at least, a representative of the Pathet Lao's political organization, the Neo Lao Haksat, which maintains two residences across from the morning market. The Pathet Lao were given seats in the 1962 coalition government but refused to take them. The delegates stayed around until 1964, when they left Vientiane; the residences, guarded by Pathet Lao soldiers, are kept for occasional visits by emissaries from Prince Souphananouvong, the leader of the Communist forces, who happens to be the half-brother of the Prime Minister Souvanna Phouma.

The enemy clearly retains a keen interest in its property, however.

Last September it protested vigorously when the Public Works Department announced its intention of building a wall around the property and also of repairing the street in front. The Pathet Lao claimed the wall would tend to isolate them from the life of the city and that in working on the street the government's steam rollers might damage their vegetable gardens. The quarrel reached the point where troops were called out to brandish guns at the guards, but in characteristic Lao fashion it gradually petered out. The wall is still unbuilt.

Vientiane's rather tolerant attitude toward cold-war politics, as reflected in its diplomatic community, is also shown in the fact that it is the principal point of entry and departure to and from Hanoi, which is the chief supplier of the Pathet Lao. The International Control Commission flies frequent flights to the North Vietnamese capital, and most of the journalists and peace-movement leaders who have been granted visas come through here. Similarly, when American prisoners of war are released, Vientiane is usually their first glimpse of the outside world. The regular European community of the city pays little attention to these comings and goings except when they involve a celebrity like the writer Mary McCarthy, for whom the French Embassy gave a reception. Representatives from the American Embassy attended, of course.

A couple of years ago, the more or less official foreigners of Vientiane were joined, unexpectedly, by a small army of hippies from Europe and America. To them, Laos seemed to offer the paradise it did to the early French: marijuana grows wild, the climate is benign, and the Laotians are as tolerant about sex as they are about most things. With their beards and beads and flowers, they came in large numbers across the Thai border—the only border by which it is possible to enter Laos by land nowadays—and settled in a section of the city called Dong Palane. The less spiritual-minded opened a colourful string of bars, the leading one of which was the Third Eye, offering cheap food, pot, rock music, and psychedelic lighting achieved by cutting holes in umbrellas that twirled on the ceiling.

Somewhat to the regret of Vientiane's other Westerners, for whom Dong Palane became a favourite place to repair after receptions, the hippies overestimated local permissiveness. Exactly why the authorities decided to clamp down is still not clear; some say it was the drugs, others that it was simply the long hair; whatever the cause, a few were expelled and most of the others apparently got discouraged and followed of their own accord.

Not, however, without certain difficulties. The Thai had become wary of the flower children long before and refused to let some of them re-enter at Nong Khai on the other side of the Mekong. Since the Laotians now refused to let them back in, they seemed doomed to a no-man's land between the two countries until some of the Vientiane embassies worked out an agreement to allow them to pass quickly through to Bangkok and out—where to, nobody is sure. Possibly to forestall any future invasions of the sort, the Laotian embassy in Bangkok now requires prospective tourists to present a letter of recommendation from their embassies along with their visa application.

The "strip" at Dong Palane continues to offer amusements, but much of its former flavour is gone in the opinion of old customers. The Third Eye, facing reality, has gone respectable and now has a sign proclaiming "All drinks one dollar" and slot machines that take nickles and dimes; it's still owned by the American black who founded it, and it still features Vietnamese rock bands, but the atmosphere is almost, if not quite, decorous.

For the less pleasant aspects of life in Vientiane—the aspects, that is, that have brought it prominence—one has to look carefully, listen to the stories in the Constellation bar, or read the Bangkok papers, which regularly report grim events that go largely unmentioned at the embassy dinners and receptions. According to these reports, for instance, the military hospitals of Vientiane are crowded with wounded soldiers from obscure battles that do not find their way into official announcements, some 80,000 refugees have fled from battle zones this year, and the Pathet Lao have control of every road leading from the capital to the provinces so that it is, in fact, isolated except by air from the rest of the country.

Some of the European diplomats consider such reports exaggerated—they remind one of how hard it is to be sure of anything in a country as deficient in communications as Laos—and a few even scoff at the notion that road travel outside of Vientiane is unsafe. "You can go anywhere you want by car," one said not long ago, adding, with a shrug, "Of course, there is a certain element of risk involved." The French ambassador's wife, a lady of singular nerve who holds a pilot's licence, says she often flies a small plane up to the Plaine des Jarres just to see who is in command of it at that particular moment.

Despite such assurances, very few Westerners do travel by road, and of those who have tried it in the recent past several have discovered that the risk was considerable. Three young American AID workers were stopped by the Pathet Lao and summarily executed not far from Vientiane four months ago, and a group of French travellers met the same fate a few months before.

An American AID employee, Loring Waggoner, who lived with his wife and family seventy miles from the capital, escaped with his life but not without a harrowing experience. When the Pathet Lao overran his house one night, he and his wife and two children managed to hide in a tunnel they had prudently built beneath the kitchen, where they stayed all night while the soldiers roamed about the house looking for him and smashing things. (Their decision to eliminate him, apparently, arose from a belief that he was a military intelligence agent.)

As a result of incidents like these, Americans in Vientiane are discouraged, if not actually forbidden, from going more than fifteen miles by road outside the city, and after dark even that limit is considered an unnecessary risk. The British diplomat who invited us to dinner on the outskirts insisted that we leave before nine o'clock, "just to be on the safe side".

The effect, on at least some, is claustrophobic. "I envy you people in Thailand," an American girl told a visitor from Bangkok. "When you want to get away for a weekend, you can just get in a car and go. Here, it reminds me of the Congo, where I used to be stationed—like being on a very small island. I think that's why so many of us stay in the compounds. If you're going to be trapped, you might as well be trapped in comfort."

In addition to being just outside the city, the Pathet Lao are generally assumed to be inside it, too, in the form of agents and sympathizers, though they have never resorted to the kind of terrorist tactics so common in Saigon. Along with them there are numerous other intelligence agents of various nationalities, giving Vientiane quite possibly the highest per capita spy population in Asia. "I suspect *everybody*," an Englishman said firmly, "and I think I'm usually right."

It is difficult to get accurate information on the military situation without actually going into the countryside, which few non-military people do. In an atmosphere in which the war is as much abstraction as reality, most of the older diplomatic residents are inclined to regard both government and Pathet Laos announcements with distinct cynicism.

But there are times when the war suddenly seems real and when a wave of jitters passes through the city. The murder of the three young Americans was one such time, and so was the ambush of the French travellers—the latter particularly so since the Europeans in the capital had previously taken it for granted that Lao hostility was directed at Americans rather than them as well. (The French, it is said, were as surprised as they were horrified by the incident.)

Tension, however, is a difficult emotion to sustain in Laos, and in the languid atmosphere of Vientiane war, death, and espionage quickly assume an air of unreality and, not infrequently, farce. Though the Laotians occasionally seem the least visible inhabitants of their capital, their distinctive philosophy pervades it; and after a few days here it is hard to reconcile what one has heard with what one sees.

The shell-scarred remains of villas and government buildings left by the savage fighting of the countercoup that drove Captain Kong Le and his paratroopers out in December 1960 have become picturesquely shrouded by tropical creepers and could easily be mistaken for the ruins of some of the eighty-odd ancient temples scattered about the city. The small, cheerful soldiers strolling about in red berets and camouflage uniforms seem on their way to a temple fair, or perhaps a fancy dress ball, rather than to a battle in which they might become one of those vague, uncertain statistics. Even torture, which according to local gossip is not unknown in Vientiane's jails for captured Pathet Lao, has a rather *outré* flavour; a favoured method of extracting information, it is said, is with the use of old-fashioned phonograph needles, and, as one resident says, "Where else on earth but Laos could you even *find* old-fashioned phonograph needles?"

A quite typical example of how things are done in Vientiane came recently when one of the Pathet Lao soldiers guarding the empty headquarters of the Neo Lao Haksat decided to defect to the government camp. (More than ten of the guards, no doubt corrupted by their surroundings, have done so in the past five years.) He did, but his defection was no hair-raising escape by night across barbed wire so common in Western cold-war melodrama. At high noon, he simply laid down his rifle, hailed a passing pedicab, and was carried in leisurely fashion off to police headquarters.

(Those phantom Pathet Laos battalions finally won, with a good deal of assistance from China and Vietnam, perhaps even from the massive bombing by those invisible Americans. Vientiane fell in 1975, in the same year as Phnom Penh and Saigon. Typically, it was a quiet surrender to inevitability; no helicopters lifting off the roof of the American Embassy while frantic would-be refugees pound at the gates. Hardship certainly followed for many people—the King, for instance, was reportedly starved to death in a remote cave, several members of the royal family (but not the resilient Prince Souvanna Phouma) retreated across the Mekong to Thailand, and numerous officials were forced into "re-education" camps, from which many of them never emerged—but there was no Khmer-Rouge-style butchery. The gates of Laos effectively closed for nearly two decades, most of the diplomats and traders went elsewhere, and the Hollywood set called KM-6, so I am told, was taken over by high-ranking Communist officials, many of them Vietnamese. Only in recent years has Vientiane started to come to life again—though still retaining its vaguely dream-like, unhurried atmosphere.)

15

ODDITIES OF THE MUSEUM WORLD

When I was about twelve years old I opened my first and only museum, in a derelict greenhouse my family let me have for the purpose. I suppose they regarded it as educational and they were right, though perhaps not in the way they expected.

Somehow I had discovered a mail order place in Chicago that specialized in scientific exhibits, and by recklessly spending all the money I had saved from birthdays, summer jobs, and other sources I managed to acquire from it the nucleus of my museum. I remember a pig embryo in formaldehyde, a stuffed bat, a tarantula mounted in a box, and some colourful insects from South America. From nearer home, I gathered a number of preserved local reptiles, some meteorites, a false eye, several pages of *Life* magazine showing the birth of a baby, and a dubious lump, presented by a veteran of the Pacific war, that was supposed to be a shrunken human head. All these I labelled imaginatively ("Blood-sucking Vampire" for the bat, I recall, and "Anyone you know?" for the head) and opened for business with a three-cent admissions charge.

Business was excellent for a week or so before a stupid little girl asked her mother about certain details in the *Life* display and brought down the wrath of the adult world. My own mother, I think, was far more shocked by the embryonic pig. In any event, the museum was closed down and I returned to my chemistry set, trying to make nitroglycerin in an upstairs closet.

Short-lived as it was, however, I feel sure this early venture was responsible for a lifelong partiality for museums that feature a touch of the bizarre along with the merely rare and beautiful. The many oddities of the Smithsonian Institution, for instance, never fail to fascinate me, and whenever I am in New York I make a point of revisiting those dinosaur eggs Roy Chapman Andrews brought back to the Museum of Natural History from the Gobi Desert. Similarly, in London I have spent hours at the Victoria and Albert contemplating that marvellous contraption known as Tippoo's Tiger.

For those who have never seen it, this consists of a nearly life-sized wooden tiger in the act of devouring an Englishman, and was found by the British at Seringapatam in 1799. According to the original description that accompanied it, the figure contains "some barrels in imitation of an Organ, within the body of the Tyger, and a row of Keys of natural Notes. The sounds produced by the Organ are intended to resemble the Cries of a person in distress intermixed with the roar of a Tyger."

The perfect museum exhibit, to my way of thinking, and I don't wonder that it is among the V&A's most popular attractions.

When I came to live in Asia, it looked as though my peculiar predilection would go largely unsatisfied. Most of the great collections in Japan, Thailand, Taiwan, and other places, as far as I could see, were firmly committed to beauty, or at least to historical significance: rare scrolls and Buddha images, splendid royal regalia, but very few pure oddities. Then gradually I began to discover the exceptions, and some of them turned out to be choice specimens indeed.

One of my early finds was the Sarawak Museum in Kuching. This should not have come as a surprise, for though today Sarawak is merely one of the states that comprise Malaysia, its history is more than ordinarily bizarre. Located on the island of Borneo, for over a century it was the private preserve of one unusual English family. James Brooke acquired it in 1841 from the Sultan of Brunei, as a reward for services rendered, and ruled it as the legendary White Rajah. Two other White Rajahs succeeded him, presiding over their kingdom from a quaint Istana overlooking the Kuching River. Their fairy-tale world collapsed in 1941 when the Japanese invaded and it never recovered, becoming first a British possession and then a part of Malaysia.

The museum was the creation of the second rajah, Charles Brooke, whose eccentricity was notable even by the high standards of Victorian England. He fiercely protected the traditions of his native Dayaks, even tolerating a bit of headhunting as long as it was not what he called "promiscuous", and encouraged his young administrators to mix freely with local girls in their lonely up-country postings. His appearance was certainly odd: having refused for some years to replace an eye lost in a hunting accident he finally did so by the simple expedient of walking into a London taxidermist and buying the first eye he saw. "It happened to be one destined for a stuffed albatross," his daughter-in-law Sylvia wrote later, "and it gave him forever afterwards the ferocious stare of some strange solitary marine bird."

His museum was based on his passionate interest in Borneo's customs and wildlife. According to Sarawak legend, it was actually designed by the Rajah's French valet; and it does indeed bear a remarkable resemblance to a huge misplaced chateau set on a slight hill overlooking Kuching's *padang*. Later curators, who included the noted anthropologist Tom Harrisson, upgraded the collection to make it one of the most respected institutions in the region; but at least when I saw it there were still a number of exhibits that clearly reflected the quirky tastes of the Rajah.

One of these, surely, was a shelf displaying the interesting items found in the stomach of a giant crocodile killed not far from Kuching, among them several buttons and a set of false teeth. Another might have been a ceremonial cup which allegedly changed colour if poison was added to its contents. And I am certain the ruler must have approved, perhaps even composed, the descriptive label for a pale-pink stuffed dolphin; after pointing out that such dolphins were common along Sarawak's coasts, the writer goes on to note that "they really are this colour, exactly like a baby's bottom".

I found an even odder museum in Brunei, the enormously rich little independent sultanate tucked away in another corner of Borneo. The money comes from oil, and apart from making the country one of the wealthiest in the world on a per capita basis, it also provides the ruler with plenty of spare cash for indulging in personal whims.

I spotted one of these as I was being driven from the airport to my hotel in Bandar Seri Begawan, the capital. We were passing a rather grandiose group of government buildings, built in the vaguely futuristic style of world's fairs, when suddenly a familiar figure loomed from a courtyard.

"Can that possibly be Winston Churchill?" I asked the driver.

"Oh yes," he replied. "And right behind it is the Churchill Museum. Only one in the world."

Whatever else Brunei might offer, I knew I was going to find satisfaction on at least one score.

It offered, as it turned out, a number of pleasing curiosities: human parking meters, for one thing, in the form of pretty girls in green uniforms who charmingly clocked cars in and out, as well as aborigines hired by the municipality to put down stray dogs with blow-guns. But the prize specimen was the Churchill Museum, built at a cost of several million dollars by the father of the present sultan.

Winston Churchill never visited Brunei, nor, apparently, did it ever loom very largely in his thoughts during his long career. Nevertheless, Sir Omar Saifuddin, whose reign saw the beginning of the sultanate's great prosperity, conceived an overwhelming admiration for the wartime leader and decided to honour his memory with a suitable edifice.

It occupies one part of a striking scimitar-shaped building that also houses an aquarium and the Brunei Historical Society. The statue I saw stands in the courtyard, a seven-foot creation complete with bowler hat and trademark cigar, one hand raised in the famous V-for-Victory salute. There is a jaunty, Chaplinesque air about the figure; if you did not immediately recognize it, you might mistake it for some music-hall comedian, caught in a celebrated routine. But the inscription on the plinth quickly banishes any such lurking levity: it expresses the stern hope that the Churchillian example will serve as "an inspired challenge to the youth of today and tomorrow".

The inspiration consists of a series of handsome exhibits put together by a British theatrical designer tracing highlights of the great man's life, starting with a scale model of Blenheim Palace where he was born and ending with huge photo-murals of his state funeral. In between are such memorabilia as a box of his favourite cigars, one of the boiler suits he favoured during World War II, and copies of all the books he ever wrote. Trip lights set off tape recordings of his famous wartime speeches, one with a clamorous counterpoint of the London blitz to heighten the effect.

The offer of blood, sweat, and tears resounds a bit strangely in the languor of Bandar Seri Begawan, but the local youth seemed to enjoy the museum as much as I did. Three shy young Dayak from the interior, clad in loin cloths, were there when I was and clapped their hands in surprised delight when the blitz barrage went off. Their favourite exhibit was a glass panel painted with scenes of the Boer War, which Churchill reported as a journalist. When a button was pushed, lights flashed and battle sounds rumbled through the airconditioned hall. The boys stood in front of it a long time, pushing the button again and again, revelling in the carnage.

Bangkok, I discovered only after living here for a long time, is full of interesting alternatives to the very proper and impressive National

Museum. Perhaps the strangest is located in the vast compound of Sirirat Hospital, across the Chao Phraya River in Thonburi. It is called the Museum of Forensic Medicine, which is appropriate since most (though by no means all) the exhibits are related to crime, with the most celebrated being a pickled murderer.

He is the main attraction for local visitors, for he occupies a lofty place in Thailand's pantheon of legendary ghouls. A Chinese by the name of Si Oey, he achieved this position back in the fifties with a series of grisly murders, all of them small children; what lifted him out of the ordinary was the fact that he cut open his victims, removed various organs, and ate them. After a much publicized manhunt, he was eventually caught and executed by firing squad.

That might have been the end of that, but Si Oey was destined to live on after death. Horror movies were based on his crimes, Thai mothers frightened their children into obedience by threatening to turn them over to his attentions, local newspapers revelled in the awful details; he was simply too famous to be quietly reduced to ashes and forgotten. So he was preserved and placed in a glass case for the edification of future generations.

And there he still stands, slightly askew, stark naked, with a sizeable hole in his chest, while visiting school girls and Buddhist monks regard him gravely, perhaps marvelling at the banality of evil. Far more unnerving, to me at least, were two other pickled murderers, unidentified, in nearby cases. Also naked, they were much larger, better preserved, and altogether more menacing than shrivelled little Si Oey.

Unfortunately, most of the museum's exhibits are unlabelled, and since there was no guide it was impossible for me to identify not only Si Oey's companions in crime but also a neat row of skulls with bullet holes, a pair of hauntingly beautiful Siamese twins in a jar, and a particularly gruesome human head that had been carefully bisected to show a bullet in the brain. (The friend who accompanied me, dauntless up until that point, took one look at the last and fled; she was still pale when I joined her outside later.)

A few, though, do bear labels of a sort, and they made me nostalgic for "Blood-sucking Vampire" and "Anyone You Know?" One consisted of an innocent-looking water jar of the sort that used to be common in every Thai bathroom, set on a low pedestal. On the wall above was a sign that said simply CONTENTS, and below that a very graphic photo of what had been found in the jar—which proved to be the assorted parts of a prominent lady chopped up by her gardener.

The other was a dusty cabinet containing a tattered little dress and a diary opened to the last faded page. The label, in Thai, explains that the dress was worn by the wife of a policeman on the night she was brutally murdered by her young lover. The diary, it goes on to point out, is a detailed record of the torrid affair, from beginning to end; the last page describes plans for the fatal final meeting.

How my greenhouse patrons would have relished that exhibit!

Sirirat also has about ten other museums, a few of them fairly routine, like a doctor's collection of prehistoric artefacts, but others decidedly outré, like one devoted to diseased organs that is really beyond any description aimed at a general audience. Elsewhere in Bangkok—and unmentioned in any guidebook I have ever come across—is the Royal Elephant Museum, devoted mostly to the sacred white variety. It contains all sorts of things bound to captivate pachyderm lovers, though my favourite (inevitably) is a portion of the skin, preserved in formaldehyde, from an especially fine specimen who tragically died during the mid-nineteenth century reign of King Rama IV. (An account of this event appears in the memoirs of Anna Leonowens, proving that she was at least accurate about some things.)

Now I am on the trail of other odd museums, described by Thai friends who have learned of my tastes. One is supposedly in a celebrated Bangkok temple and consists of a comprehensive collection of vivid photographs showing the results of terrible accidents—the purpose, so my informants say, being to suggest the transient nature of life. And the abbot of another temple just outside the city is reported to have assembled thousands of phallic objects, the largest being a ten-foot creation he himself spent several years carving.

Who knows what I may discover elsewhere in Asia? Somewhere in Vietnam, for instance, there may well be a Charles De Gaulle Museum.

16

COBRA, ANYONE?

A famous old cartoon in the *New Yorker* shows a writer for a noted news magazine, solemnly typing at a story in his office. At the line "Dog meat tastes . . ." he stops, clearly stumped. But not for long: next he is seen going into a pet shop, coming out with a plump poodle, going into a restaurant that advertises "Your Specialities Cooked to Order", and then emerging empty-handed, the staff peering after him with stricken expressions. Back at his office he confidently completes the sentence: ". . . tough and gamy".

It was in a similar spirit of dedicated research that I left my Bangkok home one evening not long ago and ventured into a shady lane a few streets away. My destination was a small restaurant set in a garden, a pleasant, almost rural-looking place if one concentrated on the rustic, thatched-roof dining area and ignored the roar of the traffic on nearby Sukhumwit Road.

There are hundreds of such places scattered through Bangkok's residential areas, and the only thing that distinguished this one from the others was the discreet sign that hung beside the entrance way. BANGKOK SNAKE HOUSE it proclaimed, and to underscore the point there was a drawing of a hooded cobra, ready to strike.

Perhaps it was an off-night for aficionados, or the fact that I had come a little later than most locals prefer to dine. In any event my Thai companion and I were the only customers, and a beaming young woman, clearly the manager, welcomed us with much enthusiasm.

"Hello, hello," she said. "You want to eat snake? We got first class cobra."

Well, yes, that was why I had come. Over my years in Thailand I had often heard about places that specialized in reptilian cuisine, but I had never gotten around to visiting any of them. For one thing, many of them offered not only snake but also what the Thais call *ahan-pha*, "wild food", meaning jungle creatures like wild boar, barking deer, and tigers. Most of these rarities are on the official list of protected species and their appearance at table in the form of spicy curries is frowned upon by the law; as a consequence, such restaurants were usually located in obscure places and not well advertised.

There *was* a snake-meat stall in Lumpini Park, right in the middle of the city, but it was only open in the very early morning when large numbers of health-minded Chinese came there to do daily exercises. Early riser though I am, the prospect of a cobra breakfast had a dim appeal at best and I never got there.

So I was able to come up with reasonable excuses for deferring the experience until one day I came across an advertisement for the Snake House in a local paper. It was open at civilized hours, it was conveniently located, it was apparently legal. There was, in short no longer any valid reason for my continuing inability to complete a sentence starting "Cobra meat tastes . . .".

"Good big cobra," the manager said, bringing a large bottle of Thai beer. She also brought a mimeographed sheet of paper to educate me on the therapeutic delights in store.

From this I learned that the gall bladder of a venomous snake was a sure-fire cure for weariness of eye-sight, high blood pressure, and constipation. "It also gives immediate result," the author added, the further to whet the appetite.

The meat "nourishes gut, intestine, liver, blood and skin complex," and also stimulates "hormone and sperm". (My Thai companion's eyes widened at the latter promise.) In addition, it was billed as an "appetizer," though I suspect something might have gone awry with the translation here. (Cobra hors d'oeuvres, on the other hand, would surely be a conversation piece at any cocktail party.)

Then there was snake oil, allegedly good for "liver, lung, trachea, eyesight, and cloudy urine", which takes in quite a lot of potential trouble spots. Finally, the place offered something called "Poison Removal Tablets", described as a "mixture of five kinds of snakes' poison and various useful plants in crude form". This remarkable concoction, according to the paper, "stimulates the cleanliness of blood, V.D., etc. . . . and eliminates various kinds of diesel in body".

I wondered whether it was a good idea to get rid of any diesel I might be harbouring, and was frankly alarmed at the prospect of V.D. stimulation; but the dedicated researcher overcame the squeamish diner.

So I said, "Yes, a cobra would be fine."

"You come choose," the owner insisted, and led us to a back area near the kitchen. There a waist-high cement trough stretched for several metres, divided into sections and covered with strong wire mesh. Peering down into the first part I saw two snakes curled in a corner, apparently asleep. As soon as an attendant pulled back the mesh, however, both reared, spread their hoods, and looked thoroughly alert.

"Which one you like?" asked the owner.

It was not exactly like choosing a lobster in one of Bangkok's many pick-it-yourself seafood restaurants, and besides, I had backed so far away I could see only the two swaying heads. "They both look nice," I said. "You choose."

She inspected the pair with a shrewd eye and finally pointed to one. "Bigger bile," she commented, somewhat mysteriously, and motioned to the attendant. Using a stick with a hook at the end, he expertly whipped my future meal out of the pit and onto the mesh of the adjoining one. There it reared and struck at thin air, flicking its tongue nastily.

Now the following step, I fear, could offend delicate sensibilities, and any reader who possesses them should perhaps skip the next couple of paragraphs. In fact, I rather wish I'd skipped watching it, though if I had I would have missed what most connoisseurs regard as the high point of the whole snake-eating experience.

Before the cobra could barely hiss a protest, it was lassooed and stretched, belly exposed. Then the attendant took a razor and made a long, deft slit, out of which popped the entrails; from these he drew the gall bladder, a greyish sac about the size of my thumb.

"Very big," the owner said proudly, as it was dropped into a small glass of warm rice wine. Meanwhile the attendant was holding a cup under the snake to catch a stream of dark-red blood; by the time the last drop had been extracted, the wine had been infused with the bile, and this was added to the blood, the bladder being set aside for another use.

This little cocktail—actually, quite a large one—is the true goal of most snake fanciers, a concentrated essence of all the reptile's curative powers, good for failing eyesight, rheumatism, and various other effects of ageing, some of which the owner indicates merely with a knowing wink. To enjoy all these benefits, one is supposed to down it in a bold gulp, with a further glass of wine, perhaps, to speed it on its way and keep it down.

I confess I failed to follow this procedure. In the interest of higher learning, I did take a tentative sip ("strong and sweetish," I duly noted); but that was all I could manage. My Thai companion, however, greatly stimulated by the mimeographed promises and that knowing wink, polished off the rest in a jiffy and suffered no ill effects. (Quite the opposite, as a matter of fact; he subsequently called to tell me he was going back for a second visit to the Snake House.)

While the cook was preparing the last part of the meal, the owner showed me a collection of take-out items for customers who want to keep handy remedies at home. Poison Removal Tablets were available, of course, large but quite innocent looking, along with dried snake meat ($25 a container), snake-bite capsules (50 cents each), and dried gall bladders (from 75 cents to $1.50 depending on the size). The latter, she explained, could be dropped "just like a tea bag" into hot water for an instant bracer.

Live cobras start at around $10 for a small specimen and pythons—non-venomous but prized for their giant gall-bladders—are about $50. The Big Daddy of them all is the king cobra, which commands as much as $500 when available, Nor is the snake's usefulness exhausted after it has been de-biled, bled, filleted, fried, and dried: the restaurant also does a brisk business in snakeskin belts, handbags, and other accessories.

At this point our cobra meat appeared stewed with a large quantity of the very hottest little Thai chili peppers, compared to which a blow torch resembles an air conditioner, and the pungent leaves of a citrus plant. Glowing bright red (from the wine, the blood, the beer, or possibly a combination of all three), my Thai companion pronounced it *aroy dee* (delicious). I myself found the chili peppers fairly overpowering, but between gasps and gulps of beer I gathered enough of an impression to be able to note, in case I should ever need it: "Cobra meat tastes hot and slightly fishy."

17

A LITERARY WINDOW ON AYUTTHAYA

L ate afternoon, after the last tourist bus has headed off to Bangkok and the last souvenir stall has shut down, is the best time to wander through the ruins of Ayutthaya, Thailand's ancient capital. The shattered temples and palaces, though spacious, are not all that impressive in the harsh light of day, at least compared to the wonders of Angkor and Pagan; only when the shadows begin to lengthen, creating mysterious pools of darkness among the stones, do they really suggest something of their former splendour and of the momentous events that took place around them.

Founded on an artificial island in the Chao Phraya River in the mid-fourteenth century, Ayutthaya was the centre of Thai power for four hundred years. It became perhaps the most magnificent city in all of Southeast Asia, larger than either London or Paris of the time, with city walls that extended for some twelve kilometres, more than ninety gates, and fifty-six kilometres of man-made waterways. Its wealth was based on trade, and trade brought a highly cosmopolitan population—Malays, Cambodians, Burmese, and Lao from neighbouring countries; Chinese, Japanese, and Indians from elsewhere in Asia; eventually the first Europeans from Portugal, Holland, Britain, and France.

In 1767, Ayutthaya fell to an invading Burmese army who proceeded to burn and loot the capital, destroying all its historical records in the process, leaving only the mute ruins of today. It is for this reason that modern historians seeking to recreate life in the city must rely chiefly on accounts by foreign visitors—in particular, by one rather special collection who all came during a short period and who, collectively, opened a rare window on this little-known kingdom.

Early Western traders and mercenaries were not literary men—some, indeed, were barely literate—and few recorded their impressions. Of those that did, many of their writings were plainly coloured by imagination, like those of a certain Captain Erwin, otherwise unidentified, who happened to meet the famous diarist Samuel Pepys in London in 1666. "The King of Siam seldom goes out without thirty or forty thousand people with him," Pepys recorded, "and not a word spoke nor a hum or cough in the whole company to be heard. [Erwin] tells me the punishment frequently there for malefactors is cutting off the crown of the head, which they do very dexterously, leaving the brains bare, which kills them presently."

By far the greatest number of accounts, and the most reliable, come from a group of visitors near the end of the seventeenth century, which also happened to be the peak of Ayutthaya's power and prosperity. They were, in the words of Maurice Collis, "the first European gentlemen of quality the Siamese had ever seen"; and nearly all wrote about their experiences, casting fresh light on a scene then almost unknown to the West.

Of the cast of notable characters involved two stand out, for without them and their strange involvement with one another, the others would not have come. Neither, as it happens, wrote anything that has survived, but they are the focus, the omnipresent stars, of all the other accounts.

One was King Narai, a somewhat anachronistic figure who came to the throne in 1656 and who managed to combine the qualities of an all-powerful, semi-divine monarch with an exceptional degree of tolerance and a strong curiosity about the outside world. The other was a sharp-witted Greek named Constantine Phaulkon ("Monsieur Constance" in many contemporary accounts) who appeared at the same time on the Ayutthaya stage.

A controversial figure during his brief moment of glory, Phaulkon remains one today; but in the complex, often impenetrable world of Thai politics he was a recognizable type to the Europeans of Ayutthaya, and this perhaps also explains why he has captivated so many Western writers over the years. "One of the most amazing of the adventurers who have made the East the scene of their exploits," observed Somerset Maugham, who in the 1920s made a special detour to visit the ruins of Phaulkon's palace at Lopburi, where King Narai often retreated for pleasure. In *Siamese White*, the story of an English freebooter named Samuel White, Maurice Collis summarizes Phaulkon as "one of those rare and fascinating youths who mature early and by their brilliance, industry, and charm captivate all who meet them. Though of formidable genius, such persons do not at first alarm, for they can combine usefulness with servility, but when their talents and guile have lifted them into power they arouse a terrified loathing in the hearts of their opponents."

One more character analysis might be useful, this from a man who wrote out of direct experience. The Chevalier Claude de Forbin was a French naval officer who modernized the forts at Bangkok in 1686 and rendered other services to Phaulkon and King Narai. He had good reason to be wary of the Greek; indeed, he suspected Phaulkon of trying to poison him to prevent his returning to France with unflattering revelations about affairs in Ayutthaya; yet he was able to see two sides to the man:

"He had high and noble aspirations: his capacity was above the average. No plan was too great for him to guide it to a successful conclusion with wisdom and circumspection. He would indeed have been fortunate if these qualities had not been marred by the most conspicuous defects, of which the chief were boundless ambition, insatiable and often sordid avarice, a jealousy which took offence at trifles and led him to be hard, cruel, and devoid of both pity and honesty."

The object of these (and many more) attempts at evaluation was born in obscurity on the island of Cephalonia, then under Venetian rule, in 1647. The family name, it seems, was Jerakis, which means "falcon" in Greek. While still a boy, perhaps ten or twelve, he went to sea aboard an English merchant ship. The next few years were spent on various ships, never rising very high in rank or amassing much in the way of material wealth but gaining valuable experiences in both European and Eastern waters; he was eventually employed by the British East India Company and, through friends made there (among them Samuel White's elder brother George), became a private trader. After being shipwrecked on the coast of southern Thailand, he arrived in Ayutthaya in 1678, unknown and powerless.

He had important assets, however. He was energetic, fluent in a number of languages, and experienced in international trade; moreover, he undoubtedly possessed considerable charm as well as a natural talent for politics and intrigue. These led to his appointment as interpreter for the powerful Barcalon, the official in charge of King Narai's trade, and soon carried him to such heights that by the time of the Chevalier de Forbin's arrival he was a confidant of the king with the title of Phra Vichayen; he had splendid palaces at Ayutthaya and Lopburi, a retinue of servants, his own private elephants, and a beautiful part-Japanese wife renowned for her culinary skills. This woman, whom he married at a church that had been built by the Portuguese, was a descendant of Japanese Catholics who had taken refuge in Ayutthaya from persecution in their homeland, and to marry her Phaulkon returned to the faith into which he had been born but from which he had strayed in his wanderings.

This is important, for he was brought back to the church by French Jesuit priests who had come to Siam some years earlier, and it was at least partly due to their influence that he embarked on the grandiose schemes that would cost him both his power and his life. The motives

that lay behind his efforts to forge an alliance between Narai's kingdom and the France of Louis XIV are tangled, however, and would
require far more space to explore in detail. Did Phaulkon really
believe, for example, as many of his Jesuit friends certainly did, that
the king (and, by extension, all the country) was ripe for conversion to
Christianity? Was he, as the conservative court mandarins thought,
setting himself up to be crowned king in a French-dominated Siam?
Was it a shrewd political move to counterbalance growing English and
Dutch influence in the region? Or was he, as most of the English residents believed, merely doing it out of an innate love of intrigue and
a desire to line his own pockets?

Whatever the reasons, King Narai decided to send three ambassadors to France. They left Ayutthaya aboard a French vessel, the
Soleil d'Orient, in 1680, carrying not only the envoys but interpreters,
attendants, a large number of gifts (including two young elephants),
and a message engraved on gold foil asking Louis XIV to send ambassadors of his own to Siam. The ship vanished without a trace somewhere between Madagascar and the Cape of Good Hope, thus fulfill-
ing prophecies of disaster by astrologers of Narai's court. A more
modest mission left in 1684 and this reached Paris safely. The two
Thai envoys made a poor personal impression, refusing to go out and
meet people, but they were received by Louis XIV in the Hall of
Mirrors at Versailles and the Sun King responded as hoped by sending an embassy the following year.

To head it, the king selected the Chevalier du Chaumont, a religious zealot who spent most of the long voyage in pious prayer.
Chaumont had been persuaded (or perhaps had persuaded himself)
that Narai was seriously contemplating conversion and that the principal object of his mission was to bring this about. He clung to this illusion throughout most of his stay, insisting on bringing up the subject
regularly in his audiences with the king. Phaulkon, who acted as his

interpreter, knew how unlikely it was that Narai would ever take such a drastic step and therefore tactfully omitted the references in his Thai translations, which no doubt created a degree of misunderstanding on both sides.

Far more sophisticated than the Chevalier was his putative assistant, the Abbé de Choisy, who in the event that the king agreed to conversion would stay behind and assist him. Well known in smart Parisian society, especially at court, Choisy had a singularly exotic past. From childhood he had been raised by his ambitious mother as a girl, complete with pierced ears and beauty patches; and he continued to be a transvestite in his youth, appearing in the highest circles as "Madame de Sancy" and charming both women and men. According to a fragmentary memoir he wrote of this period of his life, he enjoyed considerable success in the seduction of young girls and even went through a form of mock marriage with one of them, the girl dressed as a man and Choisy wearing "all my jewellery . . . and a new gown".

In 1685, when he was thirty-nine, Choisy fell seriously ill and thought he was dying. He swore to reform if he recovered and, when he did, became a fervent Catholic. It is said that he asked Louis XIV to appoint him as ambassador to Siam but that the king, who knew all about his past, declined; such was the Abbé's charm, however, that he did succeed in getting himself appointed as Chaumont's deputy.

A third member of the embassy who deserves mention was Father Guy Tachard, a Jesuit who quickly became intimate with Phaulkon and even served, for a time, as his secretary. Tachard was a schemer—the "bad character" in the story, according to historian Dirk Van der Cruyse—who plotted behind the ambassador's back and advocated French military involvement in Ayutthaya. Choisy would later write bitterly, "Chaumont and myself were but theatrical performers; the good Father was the real ambassador, in charge of the secret negotiations."

Despite these frustrations, Choisy enjoyed his stay in cosmopolitan

Ayutthaya and wrote an elegant account of his experiences in the form of letters. "We went for an excursion outside the town," he recounted. "I am never tired of admiring this very large city on an island surrounded by a river three times bigger than the Seine, full of French, English, Dutch, Chinese, Japanese, and Siamese vessels and an uncountable number of barges, and gilded galleys with sixty oarsmen. The King is beginning to build ships in the European manner; three boats have recently been launched on the waters. But something still more admirable is that on both sides of this island are the quarters or villages inhabited by the different nationalities; all the wooden houses are in the water, the buffaloes, cows, and pigs in the air [i.e., on raised floors]. The streets are alleys of fresh flowing water as far as the eye can see, under huge green trees, and in these tiny homes there is a great crowd of people. Slightly beyond the villages are the broad landscapes of rice which one passes through by boat. The rice is always above the water; and the horizon is limited by big trees, above which one sees here and there the shining towers and pyramids of the pagodas covered with two or three layers of gilding. I do not know if I am presenting your imagination an attractive view, but certainly I have never seen anything finer, though with the exception of the pagodas everything is still of natural simplicity."

The visit contained at least one moment of high comedy, according to Choisy's account. Shortly after their arrival the all-important ceremony to present Louis XIV's letter to King Narai took place at the royal palace. Phaulkon had explained that Thai kings did not accept letters from the hands of ambassadors, no matter how grand, and suggested that the document be placed in a cup at the end of a long stick and thereby lifted up to the elevated throne. Chaumont refused, saying that either the throne must be lowered or he must be provided with a platform from which he could personally deliver it; and "Monsieur Constance" finally agreed, with what one suspects was some exasperation and, knowing Thai custom, perhaps some trepidation.

"However, when we entered the room, we saw the King at a window at least six feet high. The Ambassador muttered to me, 'I cannot give him the letter at the end of a stick, and I shall never do it.' I must admit I was most embarrassed. I did not know what advice to give him. I thought of carrying the Ambassador's chair near to the throne, so that he could climb up on it, when, suddenly, after having finished his discourse, he made his decision. He moved proudly toward the throne, holding the golden cup in which was the letter, and presented the letter to the King without raising his elbow, as if the King were at the same low level as he. Monsieur Constance, who was crawling on the floor behind us, cried to the Ambassador, 'Lift it up, lift it up!' but he did no such thing, and the good King was obliged to lean half out of the window to take the letter, which he did laughing. Here is the reason. The King had told Monsieur Constance, 'I leave you to arrange everything outside, do all that is possible to honour the Ambassador of France; I shall look after the inside.' He did not wish to lower his throne, or to build a dais, and had resolved, in case the Ambassador did not raise the letter to the height of the window, to lower himself to take it."

Choisy did a little shopping, though he was disappointed at the selection ("To have rare things, you have to be here in the months of April and May, when ships arrive from China and Japan"), and was also given a tour of the royal temple where he saw a much-revered Buddha. ("The monks say this image sometimes goes for excursions outside the palace, but the desire to do so only comes when one can see nothing.") At Lopburi, King Narai's summer retreat, he and the ambassador were put up in a specially built palace with French decorative motifs and attended a hunt for wild elephants. Finally, on 15 December, after a stay of three months, they left Ayutthaya, carrying with them an enormous number of presents for the French court and three Thai envoys.

Unlike their predecessors, the Thai envoys were a social sensation in Paris, their courtly manners praised and their colourful silk costumes so admired they were soon being copied by French manufacturers. Otherwise, however, they accomplished little of substance; the real negotiations, involving the wily Tachard, were going on behind their backs and amounted to something very close to the idea of French domination in Siam, not only religious but also commercial and military.

A second embassy, led by Simon de La Loubère, a talented writer of light verse in his spare time, left for Siam in March of 1687. It was very different from Chaumont's. This time there were five ships and a total of 1,361 people, including almost 500 soldiers and 15 Jesuits led by Tachard, and instead of good will it would bring disaster to both King Narai and Phaulkon within a year.

The literary output of both voyages was remarkable. Choisy, in addition to the account already mentioned, wrote an official memorandum. Chaumont published his impressions, as did La Loubère, while Tachard and several other Jesuit priests offered their own versions of what they saw. The Chevalier de Forbin's memoirs appeared much later, in 1729, and those of a Jesuit named Père de Bèze remained unknown until 1968.

The most valuable, in the opinion of historians, was La Loubère's *A New Historical Relation of the Kingdom of Siam*, which appeared in French in 1691 and in English two years later. This is ironic in a way because as a diplomat La Loubère was not a notable success, being haughty and short-tempered, no doubt partly because of Tachard's scheming. Yet, he had a keen eye for detail, an intelligent curiosity about the customs he encountered, and recorded what he saw and heard in what remains a classic resource.

He wrote about the food, the houses, the mineral resources, the arts, the Buddhist faith, the agriculture, even the comparative charms of Thai and Burmese women. Here are his comments on the latter: "There is nothing disreputable about free love in Siamese lower-class opinion. Such love is regarded as a marriage and inconstancy as a divorce. Moreover, Siamese women have naturally such a good opinion of themselves that they do not easily yield to strangers or, at least do not solicit them. The Burmese women in Siam, as strangers themselves, suit strangers better. Some people are stupid enough to say that they are women of loose character, but the fact is that they want a husband, and when they take a European are faithful to him until he abandons them. If they have children, far from their reputation suffering, their position is assured, and that their so-called husband is white, redounds further to their reputation. It is argued by some observers, who know, that they are more amorous than the Siamese; certainly they are more sprightly and animated."

Nicolas Gervaise, who came as a missionary two years before the Chaumont embassy, was equally informative in his book *The Natural and Political History of the Kingdom of Siam*, published in 1688 and used as a source by La Loubère. He, too, discusses Thai women, in particular their curious concept of beauty:

"One thing that the Siamese ladies cannot endure about us is the whiteness of our teeth, because they believe that the devil has white teeth, and that it is shameful for a human being to have teeth like a beast's. Therefore, as soon as the boys and girls reach the age of fourteen or fifteen, they start trying to make their teeth black and shiny. They do this in the following manner: the person whom they have chosen to render them this service makes them lie down on their back and keeps them in this position for the three days that the operation lasts. First, he cleans the teeth with lemon juice and then having rubbed them with a certain fluid which makes them red, he adds a layer of burnt coconut, which blackens them. The teeth are so weakened by these drugs that they could be extracted painlessly and would even fall out if the patient risked eating any solids, so for these three days he subsists on cold soups, which are fed to him gently so that they flow down his throat without touching the teeth. The least wind could spoil the effect of this operation and that is why the patient stays in bed and makes sure that he is well covered until he feels that it is successfully accomplished by the teeth regaining their firmness in the gums and the disappearance of the swelling of the mouth, which resumes its normal proportions."

Tachard wrote two books—*Voyage de Siam des Pères Jesuites* in 1688 and *Second Voyage* in 1689—and while he was discreet about his backstage role, he seems just as fascinated as the others by the usual sights he encountered; he includes a lengthy and detailed account of the wild-elephant hunt staged by King Narai for the amusement of his visitors.

The La Loubère mission arrived in September 1687 and left at the end of December, having signed a commercial treaty at the king's palace in Lopburi. French troops remained behind at forts that had been built on either side of the river at Bangkok, under orders from Phaulkon to hurry to Ayutthaya in case of trouble.

Phaulkon had good reason to be concerned. Much had happened in the capital during the three years between the two French embassies. A plot to overthrow King Narai had been discovered and put down, and anti-foreign sentiment was rising in conservative circles. In March the king fell desperately ill and the next month open rebellion erupted, led by the Commander of the Royal Regiment of Elephants. Phaulkon could probably have escaped to the comparative safety of Bangkok but chose to go instead to his palace in Lopburi, where he was arrested, tortured for more than a month, and, on June 6, beheaded on the shore of a nearby lake. Narai in due course died and was replaced by the rebel leader.

There are various accounts of Phaulkon's death, each reflecting the prejudices of the writer. One is in *Histoire de Monsieur Constance*

by a Jesuit priest named Père d'Orléans, published in 1690, so roman-
tically embellished that one later historian suggested a better title
might be "Eulogy of a Fictitious Martyr". But the *Histoire* was widely
read, both at the time and much later: Somerset Maugham, for example, used it as source when he wrote his travel book about Burma and
Thailand, and so did Anna Leonowens in her famous memoir.

One Jesuit account that did not see publication during his lifetime,
or, indeed, for more than two-and-a-half centuries after his death, was
written by Père de Bèze, who came with Tachard in the second mission. He stayed in Siam for fourteen months, long enough to become
close to Phaulkon and to witness the revolution; on his way home
after being expelled, he fell prisoner to the Dutch, then at war with
France, and did not reach Paris until 1691.

By that time Tachard and d'Orléans had already published their
versions of the events in Siam. Evidently, however, de Bèze's religious
superior wanted further information, and so asked the priest to put
down his own recollections, not for public view but merely for the
Jesuit files. De Bèze seems to have been a little surprised by the
request—in his foreword he suggests that he has "little to relate with
which Your Reverence is not familiar"—but he complied with it,
drawing partly on what Phaulkon had told him and partly what he had
seen for himself.

The de Bèze memoir, together with other documents related to
Siam—one of them a letter from Phaulkon to Tachard in
Portuguese—remained with the Jesuits until the order was sup-
pressed in France following the Revolution. Thereafter it disappeared and did not emerge until 1917 in, of all places, Peking, where
it formed part of the estate of a noted English collector, Dr. G.E.
Morrison. All the documents were then purchased by a Japanese
bibliophile, the Baron Iwasaki, and taken to Tokyo.

It was there that they were examined in 1936 by an Englishman named E.W. Hutchinson, who was researching a book about foreign adventurers in Siam. Hutchinson was not a writer by profession; most of his working life had been spent in the country's northern provinces, first with the Forestry Department of the Thai Government and later with a British trading company. He became fascinated, however, by the colourful cast of characters who had assembled in seventeenth-century Ayutthaya and uncovered a number of previously unknown documents relating to them. One, which he found at the library of the French Foreign Mission in Paris, was an anonymous manuscript by "An English Catholic", written expressly to refute the glowing portrait of Phaulkon in d'Orléans' *Histoire* and giving a very different version of the Greek's personal history and activities in Siam. Another was the de Bèze memoir which, while flattering to Phaulkon, was also far more outspoken and factual than other known Jesuit works on the subject.

The publication of *Siamese White* in 1936 must have come as a shock to Hutchinson. Maurice Collis, who had worked for many years as a British civil servant in Burma, had a talent for popular history and his book enjoyed a considerable success. Hutchinson's proposed work, dealing with many of the same events and characters, could only suffer as a result. Nevertheless, he decided to go ahead and *Adventurers in Siam in the Seventeenth Century* appeared in 1940, just in time to face an even worse handicap in the form of World War II; after a single edition, it went out of print until a new one was issued by a Bangkok firm in 1985.

Hutchinson's interest continued, however, and after the war he was able to obtain a complete transcription of Père de Bèze's memoir, made by two French scholars in Tokyo. This he translated and published in 1968 as *Revolution in Siam*, at last bringing the Jesuit's narrative to public light.

De Bèze proved not only a meticulous recorder of events he saw at first hand but also a gifted storyteller, happily free from melodramatic flourishes. By way of illustrating this, one may compare his account of Phaulkon's death with that of Anna Leonowens, who relied partly on d'Orléans and partly on her own vivid imagination.

Anna claims with absolute assurance, but total inaccuracy, that King Narai committed suicide just before he was to be assassinated. Then: "Turning from the corpse of the king, the baffled regicides dashed to the luxurious apartment where Phaulkon slumbered, as was his custom of an afternoon, unattended save by his fair young daughter Constantia. Breaking in, they tore the sleeping father from the arms of his agonized child, who with piteous imploring offered her life for his, bound him with cords, dragged him to the woods beyond his garden, and there, within sight of the lovely little Greek chapel he had erected for his private devotions, first tortured him like fiends, and then, dispatching him, flung his body in a pit. His daughter, following them, clung fast to her father, and, though her heart bled and her brain grew numb between the gashes and the groans, she still cheered him with passionate endearments; and, holding before his eyes a cross of gold that always hung on her bosom, inspired him to die like a brave man and a Christian."

Rather different, and probably closer to the truth, is the de Bèze version (which also gives the correct sex of Phaulkon's child):

"The courtier came for him at the appointed hour and conducted him on the back of an elephant to the place outside the city which Phetracha [the new king] had chosen for his execution. Having dismounted Constance went down on his knees—so the courtier informed us—and made protest before God in whose Presence he would soon be standing, that he died innocent of the crimes imputed to him by Phetracha; that the motive of his every action had been to serve and magnify the King, likewise to maintain the throne in the interest of the Royal Family. He then entreated the courtier to have a care for his wife and son, also to protect the poor Christians suffering persecution without just cause. He handed to the courtier the Cross of the Order of St. Michael, requesting him to conserve it for his son until such time as the boy will be of age to carry it for himself as a token of the French king's liking for his father.

"He then put forth his neck beneath the 'Red Arm,' who swung the executioner's sword down upon it with a mighty stroke and then with a backstroke laid open his stomach—as is the custom for those beheaded."

The literary window so briefly opened now effectively closed. Siam never actually sealed itself off from foreigners, as Japan tried to do, but the number dwindled to a mere trickle after 1688. The Dutch, because of their hostility to the French, were able to keep their factory open and one of their countrymen, Engelbert Kaempfer, passed through in 1690 on his way to Japan; through him we catch a tantalizing glimpse of Phaulkon's widow, who with her young son had been reduced to begging from door to door and, according to Kaempfer, was bitter toward the memory of the husband who had brought her to such a low estate. (This part of the story, at least, has a happy ending; she eventually became part of the royal kitchen, where she is credited with introducing many sugary egg-based sweets that are still popular in modern Thailand.)

But it was not for over a century, after Bangkok became the capital, that the West would get another close view of the exotic kingdom through the printed page.

18

MAUGHAM IN SIAM

In November of 1922, an English-language newspaper in Bangkok informed its readers that "Mr. Somerset Maugham, novelist and playwright, has arrived at Rangoon from Ceylon with the intention of making a prolonged tour in the Shan States, crossing the Salween River, and eventually making his way via Chiang Mai to Bangkok".

Maugham was already a famous literary figure at the time. He had written such popular novels as *Lisa of Lambeth* and *Of Human Bondage*, as well as a series of successful plays (four were running simultaneously at one time on the London stage) and had also travelled to such remote places as China and Tahiti, gathering material for future books. This was his first visit to South Asia, his only one to Siam (as it was then known), and his last until a farewell tour toward the end of his life.

Malaya and Borneo would become the background for some of his most famous stories. Perhaps he had similar hopes for Burma and Thailand, but if so they never materialized. What resulted instead was *The Gentleman in the Parlour*, his only pure travel book, which was not published until 1930. It went through several editions but was only a moderate success compared to most of his other work and did not became generally available again until a reprint was issued in 1995.

His companion on the trip (who is nowhere mentioned in the book) was a young man named Gerald Haxton, who served as a sort of secretary-companion. Their original plans were vague and did not include the little-known Shan States of northern Burma. On the ship from Colombo, however, they happened to meet a man who had spent five years in Keng Tung, the principal city of the region, and praised its charms. "It had pagodas darkly splendid and a remoteness that liberated the questing spirit from its anxiety. I asked him what it had offered him and he said, contentment."

That was enough to pique the curiosity of the two travellers, who on arrival in Rangoon set about making plans for a journey that promised to be extraordinarily difficult and, indeed, remains so today. They went by steamer up the Irrawaddy to Pagan and Mandalay, by train to Thazi, by car to Taunggyi, and by pony to Keng Tung, crossing the Salween on the way. He dallied for a while in Keng Tung, not apparently finding the sort of contentment his shipboard acquaintance had promised ("It was a village, larger than those I had passed on the way, but a village notwithstanding"), but admiring the colourful tribes who gathered at the market; after resting for a week, he mounted his pony again for another long trek through dense jungle to the "small, sluggish stream" that formed the border of Siam. A few more days of hard travel ensued before "quietly, like the anti-climax of play" he emerged from wild countryside to find a red Ford waiting for him in the shade of a palm tree.

"It was the first car in the history of man that had ever passed that way," he mused as he drove down a bumpy track the next morning, "and the peasants in their fields looked at us in amazement. I wondered whether it occurred to any of them that in it they saw the symbol of a new life. It marked the end of an existence they had led since time immemorial. It heralded a revolution in their habits and their custom. It was a change that came upon them panting and puffing, with a slightly flattened tyre but blowing a defiant horn, Change."

At sunset they reached another sort of coming revolution, the extremity of the northern railway line: "There was a new, gaudily-painted resthouse at the station; and it might almost have been called a hotel. There was a bathroom, with a bath you could lie down in, and on the veranda long chairs in which you could loll. It was civilization."

Forty-eight hours now stretched between them and Bangkok, but there were two further stops he planned to make before his destination. One was Lopburi, where he wanted to see what remained of the palace of Constantine Phaulkon (which Maugham spells Faulkon), a seventeenth-century Greek adventurer who had sought to forge an alliance between Siam and France. This, however, proved a disappointment—". . . of the grand house which he built nothing remains but the high brick walls that surrounded it and three or four roofless buildings, crumbling walls and the shapes of doors and windows. They still have the vague dignity of the architecture of Louis XIV. It is an unhandsome ruin that reminds you of nothing but a group of Jerry-built villas destroyed by fire."

(Maugham drew most of his information about Phaulkon from a highly unreliable account written by a Jesuit priest named Père d'Orléans. It contains a report of how, after the Greek's death, his part-Japanese Catholic wife courageously defended her virtue from the onslaughts of a Siamese prince, constantly urged toward the glory of martyrdom by her eighty-eight-year-old grandmother. Of this dramatic scene, Maugham wryly comments: "It is satisfactory to learn that, sustained by these counsels and fortified by the incessant admonitions of the Jesuit fathers, the widow resisted all temptations to become the bejewelled inmate of an almost royal seraglio and ended her virtuous days as a dishwasher in the house of a gentleman of no social consequence.")

His other intended stop was the old capital of Ayutthaya, but after the discouraging views of Lopburi he decided to satisfy his curiosity about this ancient city from the comfort of his railway carriage: "After all if a man of science can reconstruct a prehistoric animal from its thigh bone why cannot a writer get as many emotions as he wants from a railway-station?" Moreover, he was tired of the discomforts of rest-houses, the tinned food, the absence of any mail from home, and eager for "the modest comfort of an Eastern hotel". He had not reckoned, though, on the determination of a young man assigned to serve as his guide, who promptly unloaded his luggage and carried him off despite all protests.

An exhausting tour followed. Maugham was shown "innumerable heads of Buddha in bronze and stone", vast ruined pagodas and royal palaces, a few temples that were still crowded with worshippers; at last, at the end of a long hot day, he was installed in a houseboat on the river bank, and here at last he found the solitude he craved: "When I awoke in the night I felt a faint motion as the houseboat rocked a little and heard a little gurgle of water, like the ghost of an Eastern music travelling not through space but through time. It was worth while for that sensation of exquisite peace, for the richness of that stillness, to have endured all that sightseeing."

The next day he and Haxton were in Bangkok, where they were promptly handed a card by a street tout that read: "Oh, gentleman, sir, Miss Pretty Girl welcome you Sultan Turkish bath, gentle, polite, massage, put you in dreamland with perfume soap. Latest gramophone music. Oh, such service. You come now! Miss Pretty Girl want you, massage you from tippy-toe to head-top, nice, clean, to enter Gates of Heaven."

Miss Pretty Girl stood little chance of success with either man, but in Maugham's case, besides the obvious obstacle, there was another, much more serious one, announced by the local paper on January 10: "We regret to learn that Mr. W. Somerset Maugham is down with malaria fever, doubtless contracted when coming overland from Mandalay. His temperature this afternoon was 103."

It was a severe attack. Lying in the comfort of his room at the Oriental Hotel, his temperature "soared to those vertiginous heights that are common in malaria and neither wet sheets or ice packs brought it down". At one point his condition seemed so serious that he overheard Madame Maria Maire, the German manageress, talking urgently to the doctor on the verandah outside his room. "I can't have him die here, you know," she said. "All right," the doctor replied. "But we'll wait a day or two yet." To which Madame Maire replied, "Well don't leave it too long." As we shall see, this incident was not forgotten and Maugham chose another hotel when he came on his final visit in 1959.

Perhaps because of his illness, his initial reactions to the Siamese capital were less than favourable. "Bangkok," he observed. "I put my impressions on the table, as a gardener puts the varied flowers he has cut in a great heap, leaving them for you to arrange, and I ask myself what sort of pattern I can make out of them. For my impressions are like a long frieze, a vague tapestry, and my business is to find in it an elegant and at the same time moving decoration. But the materials that are given to me are dust and heat and noise and whiteness and more dust." New Road, the main street, was "lined with houses, low and sordid, and shops, and the goods they sell, European and Japanese for the most part, look shop-soiled and dingy". Chinatown was "a network of small streets, dark, shaded, and squalid, and tortuous alleys paved with cobble stones". He could find nothing at first that made it different from all the other modern cities of the East "with their straight streets, their arcades, their tramways, their dust, traffic, their ceaseless din".

Even the broad avenues of the newer parts of the city, inspired by those of European capitals, he found wanting. "They are handsome, spacious and stately, shaded by trees, the deliberate adornment of a great city devised by a king ambitious to have an imposing seat; but they have no reality. There is something stagy about them, so that you feel they are more apt for court pageants than for the use of every day.

No one walks in them. They seem to await ceremonies and processions. They are like the deserted avenues in the park of a fallen monarch."

Even so, he sensed that there was more to Bangkok and the other great Asian cities: "When you leave them it is with a feeling that you have missed something and you cannot help thinking that they have some secret that they have kept from you. And though you have been a trifle bored you look back on them wistfully; you are certain that they have after all something to give you which, had you stayed longer or under other conditions, you would have been capable of receiving. For it is useless to offer a gift to him who cannot stretch out a hand to take it."

As his health improved, though, he was able to receive a few of these tantalizing gifts. The city's numerous Buddhist temples, for example, which most sophisticated European visitors found a bit over-decorated, came as a revelation to Maugham: "They are unlike anything in the world, so that you are taken aback, and you cannot fit them into the scheme of the things you know. It makes you laugh with delight to think that anything so fantastic could exist on this sombre earth. They are gorgeous; they glitter with gold and whitewash, yet are not garish; against that vivid sky, in that dazzling sunlight, they hold their own, defying the brilliancy of nature and supplementing it with the ingenuity and the playful boldness of man. The artists who developed them step by step from the buildings of the ancient Khmer had the courage to pursue their fantasy to the limit; I fancy that art meant little to them, they desired to express a symbol; they knew no reticence, they cared nothing for good taste; and if they achieved art it is as men achieve happiness, not by pursuing it, but by doing with all their heart whatever in the day's work needs doing."

One temple in particular, Wat Suthat, inspired him to a flight of near poetry: "The square columns, fluted at the corners, slope slightly inwards, and their capitals are strange upspringing flowers like flowers in an enchanted garden. They give the effect of a fantastic filigree of gold and silver and precious gems, emeralds, rubies, and zircons. And the carving on the gable, intricate and elaborate, droops down like maidenhair in a grotto, and the climbing snake is like the waves of the sea in a Chinese painting. The doorways, three at each end are very tall, are of wood heavily carved and dully gilt, and the windows, close together and high, have shutters of faded gilt that faintly shines. With the evening, when the blue sky turns pink, the roof, the tall steep roof with its projecting eaves, gains all kinds of opalescent hues so that you can no longer believe it was made by human craftsmen, for it seems to be made of passing fancies and memories and fond hopes."

He was charmed, too, by a tour of the city's *klong* (canals) which, as he observed "gives Bangkok its individuality". They reminded him of London streets, with the Chao Phraya River serving as the main highway and one of the main *klong* as Oxford Street, lined on both sides with "houseboats on which are shops open to the river front, and people go about making their purchases in sampans. Some of the canals are so broad that pontoons are moored in mid-stream and thus make a double or a treble row of shops. Little steamers, the omnibuses of the thrifty, puff up and down quickly, crowded with passengers; and as the rich in their great cars splash the passersby on a rainy day in London, so opulent Chinamen in motorlaunches speed along with a wash that makes the tiny dugouts rock dangerously."

Having arrived in Bangkok by an unconventional route, Maugham and Haxton chose one almost as unusual for their departure; they took "a shabby little boat of four or five hundred tons" to a seaside resort called Kep, on the Cambodian coast, went from there by car to Phnom Penh and Angkor Wat, and then by river steamer along the Mekong to Saigon.

Maugham came back to Thailand, as Siam was then called, in the winter of 1959–60. Gerald Haxton had died, of tuberculosis, during the Second World War and now there was a new secretary-companion named Alan Searle, whose duties in Bangkok consisted mostly of finding partners with whom the elderly writer could enjoy a game of bridge. These games started and ended early, one participant still remembers: "Around nine thirty or ten Alan would say 'Time for bed, Willie', and hurry him back to his hotel; then Alan would go out to sample Bangkok's much-acclaimed nightlife." His hotel this time was the new government-owned Erawan; memories of Madame Maire's long-ago consultation with the doctor outside his room at the Oriental were still sharp.

On 25 January 1960, shortly before his departure, he was given an eighty-sixth birthday party at Chulalongkorn University's Faculty of Arts, where a delegation of students blessed him by pouring scented lustral water over his hands.

He described himself to an interviewer from a local paper as an "extinct volcano". But he was not quite extinct. He lived on for five more years, published another book (a vicious attack on his ex-wife Syrie, which lost him many of his remaining friends) and finally died on 15 December 1965.

19

THE SLIGHTLY MAD CHARM OF THE REAL BANGKOK

On 4 July 1946, some 60 people turned up for an Independence Day reception given by the newly-appointed American ambassador to Thailand in the rather ramshackle quarters that then served as both embassy and residence. This gathering—mostly missionary families, together with a handful of businessmen, embassy staffers, and military personnel left over from the war—constituted almost the entire American community at the time.

If such a party were held today (the custom was stopped a number of years ago) the now spacious grounds of the ambassador's residence on Wireless Road would have to accommodate a mob of between eight and ten thousand, the largest colony of Americans living anywhere in Southeast Asia with the possible exception of the Philippines. A third of them, perhaps, have been posted there by the foreign service, the United Nations, or multi-national firms. But the great majority are residents by choice, who have come to think of Thailand as home.

They can be found in almost every conceivable occupation. There are American bankers, lawyers, doctors, teachers, journalists, architects, and management consultants. A number grow rice and other crops on land owned by Thai women they married during the Vietnam War. At any given time, a few dozen are Buddhist monks, going out each morning in their saffron robes to receive food from the faithful. Neat, clean-cut young Americans, always in pairs, walk the streets of Bangkok handing out pamphlets on behalf of The Church of Jesus Christ of Latter-day Saints. Others, not so clean-cut, operate bars and

discos in the bawdy Patpong and Soi Cowboy areas. A chef from
Louisiana dispenses gumbo and jambalaya at a place called Bourbon
Street. Still others design dresses, sell Thai silk, deal in star sapphires,
and, from time to time, occupy Thai jails as convicted drug smugglers.

What keeps so many Americans in a relatively remote country that
offers no alluring tax advantages, has a language notoriously difficult
to master, and, as any veteran of the immigration department can
attest, does not exactly welcome new residents with open arms?

In the case of missionaries, monks, and prisoners, the answers are
obvious. It may be more difficult to explain why others are here, particularly those of us who choose to live in Thailand's chaotic capital
city. We have grown accustomed to visitors who take one, or sometimes two, looks at Bangkok and finally muster up the courage to ask,
in frank dismay, "But how can you *live* in such a place?"

When I attempt to view the city through their eyes, I can see what
they mean. Mile after mile of shoddily built row shops and what are
euphemistically called "town houses" (though most of them soon
become shops, too) peel and crack only a few years after they go up.
Gaping potholes in the streets and sidewalks are often large enough
to swallow up unwary pedestrians and now and then a hapless *tuk-tuk*
(three-weeled, motorized taxi). Jagged glass atop high walls turns the
homes of the wealthy into mini-fortresses. Everywhere are unsightly
electric wires, stunted trees, and piles of litter from vendors the city
government has been ordering off the sidewalks for years. No: whatever the Tourism Authority may try to suggest, Bangkok is not a
lovely city.

Its traffic jams and pollution are legendary, even by the deplorable
standards of other Asian capitals. When Saigon fell in 1975, there was
a standing joke that if the Vietnamese ever invaded the country they
would be stopped dead in their tank tracks upon reaching the outskirts of Bangkok. And to judge from the front pages of the local

press, one would think horrendous crimes are so commonplace they scarcely deserve the lurid headlines evoking mass murder, official corruption, innocent girls sold into prostitution, and jealous wives who mutilate their husbands in ways too fiendish to describe—though they *are* described, and often depicted, too.

"If must have been very different when you came," visitors say hopefully. Those of us who now qualify as old-timers usually agree it was, just to change the subject.

But actually it wasn't, at least not when I moved here in 1960. Even then, with vast slums in many of the sites now occupied by shophouses and the streets in even worse condition than they are today, Bangkok was scarcely beautiful. There were fewer private cars and more of the *klong* (canals) that arouse such nostalgia today; but snail's-pace pedicabs made driving just as much of a nightmare, and most of the *klong* were mere oily trickles, reeking of garbage and dead things. (My first dining room overlooked a *klong*, and I grew so accustomed to its smell I was surprised by guests who turned pale when a summer breeze wafted its full potency over the table.) And one of the very first Thai words I learned was *kamoy*, which means "burglar"— in plentiful supply then as now.

So, flaws acknowledged, why do so many of us prefer Bangkok to Americanized Manila, law-abiding Tokyo, and squeaky-clean Singapore?

Any answer must necessarily be a personal one, since motives vary as much as human nature. I have heard fellow expatriates give reasons as mundane as making money and as exotic as spiritual proximity to a dead husband. Under the influence of drink, an English friend blurted out his at an embassy dinner party. "And what has kept you here for so long?" a gracious, titled lady asked him politely. At that point there was a lull in the general conversation, so everyone heard his instinctively honest reply: "Sex."

My own love affair with Bangkok began when I came on a visit back in 1959. *The King and I* was the extent of my knowledge of the place, and it took only a few days to dispel the romantic aura cast by that lovely fantasy. Yet I was immediately beguiled by the peculiar charms of the real Bangkok, which were somehow embodied for me in the hotel where I stayed for most of my visit.

A single night in the venerable old Oriental Hotel convinced me I would quickly have to find a cheaper place, and for assistance I turned to Jim Thompson of Thai silk fame, to whom I had a letter of introduction. Today, when I consider how I react to total strangers who call with similar requests, I can only marvel at the kindness shown me by Jim and many others on that first trip. Perhaps because visitors were fewer then, they were welcomed as novelties; or perhaps Jim was merely more generous than I with his time. In any event, he booked me into an establishment called the Coronet, overlooking Lumpini Park, with a standing invitation to dine at the little house where he then lived on the other side of the park.

The Coronet was odd in almost every respect, starting with the architecture, which made the maximum use of a very narrow strip of land between a *klong* and a busy lane. It consisted of a long row of box-like rooms, precariously cantilevered over the lane so that the traffic rumbled past literally under one's bed and often shook the whole structure. To most of the guests, this made little difference, for few of them were there to sleep. The Coronet, not to mince words, was what is known as a "short-time" hotel, meaning that the little rooms were generally rented out by the hour to romantic couples who had often met in the nearby park. As a result, the traffic in and out of them was frequently busier than that on the street below.

I spent nearly a month at the Coronet, perhaps the longest-staying guest it ever knew. In later years, after I came to live in Bangkok, older members of the staff used to call out greetings whenever I passed, and once I heard one of them remark to a junior employee, with a certain awe, "That's the one who got mail."

At first I viewed the hotel as simply a rather bizarre bit of local colour. It offered a steady stream of experiences that were not always pleasant but that were certainly never dull: earthquake-like tremors when trucks passed beneath, nearly grazing the floor; midnight knocks and mysterious telephone calls, rarely for me; an attempted murder in the room next to mine; and once, a police raid that revealed me to be the only guest alone in his bed. (The officer in charge was both puzzled and sympathetic.) Gradually, though, I came to perceive the Coronet as a reflection of the confused and sprawling city that sur- rounded it—distorted, of course, like the images in a fun-house mir- ror, but nonetheless containing an essential element of truth. Bangkok, too, is bizarre, a little mad, and full of surprises both serendipitous and not. Also like the Coronet, it is never dull. When I left after that first visit I knew I had to come back for a longer stay.

When I did I had no real plans to remain permanently, and in that I think I was typical of most Americans (and other Westerners) who live here. A few months became a year, then a decade; suddenly, almost without realizing it, one was an old-timer. What continued— and continues—to hold me, apart from such things as close friends and work, is that same general air of unpredictability, of chaos just around the corner, that made life at the Coronet a constant adventure.

Almost nothing in Bangkok goes quite the way it was planned or is quite what it seems. Here the unexpected is the norm. At a fashion show staged for an extremely serious conference of the International Women's Club—don't even ask why they had a fashion show at all— the elegant models turned out to be transvestites. When I invited the American and French ambassadors to a grand (and, for me, very untypical) dinner party one night, it turned into low farce; the heav- ens opened to deposit the heaviest rain in a decade, all the lights went out, one of the ambassadorial cars went into a drainage ditch, and in the dark the cook mistook salt for sugar. Nor are state visitors immune to Bangkok's capricious character. Queen Elizabeth's limousine broke down during another rainstorm in the middle of a street, necessitating her damp transfer to another. (Red ants also fell down the back of her dress at a picnic, but that happened up in Chiang Mai so perhaps doesn't count.)

The chaotic nature of the city sometimes has an unfortunate effect on would-be expatriates. I once watched a nice American family who lived near me go slowly to pieces. The husband took to muttering incoherently about the way people drove and did business, the teenaged son discovered drugs and Patpong bar girls, and the wife, who worried obsessively about snakes and germs, finally broke one afternoon and ran down the street stark naked. They were quickly shipped home, where, I was told, they soon resumed their normal, placid life.

Others, like Carol Hollinger, have found Bangkok a stimulating revelation. She came to Thailand in the mid-fifties with her husband, a foreign-service officer, and quickly despaired of the social life led by most diplomatic wives. So she got a job teaching at Chulalongkorn University, plunged happily into the local scene, and later produced a book called *Mai Pen Rai Means Never Mind*, which is probably the best account of what it is really like to live in Bangkok.

Carol Hollinger found the city's confusion exhilarating: "To me it was wild adventure to set out to a mundane party or on an innocent errand and to end up five hours later lost, hot, tired, and desperate. I admit it doesn't sound like fun and it never was comfortable, but it was in those hot and hectic moments that I was most intensely aware that I had shed suburbia."

For the first time in her life, she even found driving fun: "You had to be intensely alert to avoid collision and you were not frantically bored by regimented multitudes all obeying the law rigidly and stopping because they saw red and green. Driving was creative in Thailand."

Unlike most other writers on the subject, she scarcely mentions the great tourist attractions: the fabled temples and palaces, Thai classical dancing, the museums and art collections. She was aware of them, of course—they added to the general exotic tone of the place—but it was the vital, vivid texture of daily life that really enraptured her.

I never met Carol Hollinger. She left the university a year before I joined the staff and died suddenly just after she wrote her book. But I am sure we would have gotten along splendidly because the qualities that appealed to her are largely those that hold me.

I like, for instance, the messy, carefree way a major part of Bangkok's life takes place on its sidewalks, undeterred by withering sun, clamorous traffic, or monsoon deluge. Thais are inveterate sidewalk snackers, and there must be a million establishments of varying size meeting the urgent need for a bowl of spicy noodles, a slice of sugared guava, or a glass of iced coffee thick with sweet condensed milk. Most of them are illegal—for Bangkok residents love breaking the law almost as much as they love snacking—and stalls spring up anywhere a potential clientele is perceived to exist.

One such establishment appeared outside the gate of a house I once rented to cater to the needs of workers at a private hospital next door. At first it consisted simply of a portable noodle stand that a jolly woman wheeled up every morning. Then it gradually expanded, week by week, until eventually it had six tables with stools and sunshades and filled a good quarter of the narrow road. There were frequent traffic jams. Once an ambulance got stuck, and the patient had to be carried on a stretcher the rest of the way, past snacking nurses. But it became such a part of the neighbourhood that nobody would have dreamed of trying to get rid of it, least of all the policeman who lunched there daily.

Some *have* dreamed of getting rid of the sidewalk vendors who clog the streets leading to every important market in the city. These are also mostly illegal, and just about every municipal administration has attempted to control them during a brief fervor of law enforcement. All their efforts have been dismal failures, however, for the good and obvious reason that it is fun as well as economical to stall-shop, pausing to pick over a pile of jeans here, or a display of jogging shorts there. The only way an ordinary shop could hope to create such exhilaration would be to duplicate the sidewalk conditions as nearly as possible. In fact, by stacking goods haphazardly in narrow aisles and holding endless sales, several of the more successful Bangkok department stores have done precisely that.

I also derive joy from the imaginative use of English, as revealed not only in my morning *Bangkok Post* and the menus of both humble and grand establishments but also in signs glimpsed along otherwise drab streets. "Charming hostages can provide more of what you have expected," once promised a new domestic airline. "Peanus salad and Fried Etc." are offered by a Cantonese establishment, "Boston Scotch Sundae" by an icecream parlor, and, one memorable Christmas, "Roast Stuffed Uncle Tom Turkey" by the Siam Intercontinental Hotel. A coffee shop, alas now gone, advertised "a tasty treat waiting for you inside the Puberty Cafe". And it delights me to know that I can have clothes made at tailor shops called the Cheap Habbit, the Supper Fair, the West Size, and the Sexy.

Even the much-maligned shophouses have a zany kind of beauty if one is willing to see it. Their colours are as gaudy as a Carmen Miranda costume, and their manic architectural flourishes defy the laws of gravity as well as common sense. At about two metres wide for the whole of its considerable length, one shop house rivals the Coronet for its use of available space. Another, best viewed from a nearby overpass, has a lush roof garden with brilliant bougainvillea, full-grown trees, and a five-tier Chinese pagoda. Yet another, not far from where I live, has an enormous cage on the roof filled with hundreds of white peacocks.

Geoffrey Gorer, a visitor in the thirties, wasn't amused by such architectural follies. "It is very difficult to take Bangkok seriously," he wrote severely. "It is the most hokum place I have ever seen, never having been to California. It is the triumph of the 'imitation' school; nothing is what it looks like; if it's not parodying European buildings it is parodying Khmer ones; failing anything else it will parody itself."

(Another visiting writer, who *had* been to California, took a more generous view. "From the very beginning," wrote S.J. Perelman in *Westward Ha!*, "I was charmed by Bangkok . . . . Its character is complex and inconsistent; it seems at once to combine the Hannibal, Missouri of Mark Twain's boyhood with Beverly Hills, the Low Countries, and Chinatown.")

An American woman I used to know here would never have seen (or heard) the white peacocks on the shophouse roof. She lived in a fully airconditioned house, and her airconditioned car had tinted windows that shut out the glare and much of the view. Nor, as far as I know, did she ever brave the sidewalk vendors outside Pratunam Market, lie in a deck chair watching the kite fights at Sanam Luang outside the walls of the Grand Palace, eat noodles by a stinking *klong*, get lost in the crowded alleyways of Chinatown, spend an hour or two at the noisy shrine to Brahma near the Grand Hyatt Erawan Hotel on the night before the national lottery is drawn, or visit a restaurant that specializes in cobra meat. I doubt if she ever *heard* of the Coronet Hotel.

But it was probably just as well. Although she was not a dull, unimaginative person, fearful of foreign experiences—she had lived happily in Japan—she was not the Bangkok type.

Those of us who are Bangkok types usually recognize it early on—often, as in my case, after only a few days. At least one old-timer I know sensed it long before he even came to the city. Somehow, in the California town where he was studying, he saw a copy of the *Bangkok Post* back in the late forties. It contained a story that struck an immediate chord in him. A tram car, it seems, had hit a pedicab, which thereupon rammed a taxi, which swerved and fell into a canal on top of a charcoal boat. "I decided then and there," he told me, "that I had to live in a place where such marvellous accidents could happen."

A taste for anarchy draws some, an attraction to the culture, others; but nearly all Western expatriates who love Bangkok have an odd, satisfying sense of being where they belong. Somerset Maugham touched on the feeling in *The Moon and Sixpence*, his novel based on the life of Paul Gauguin, who also found happiness in a strange place:

"I have an idea [the narrator observes] that some men are born out of their due place. Accident has cast them amid certain surroundings, but they always have a nostalgia for a home they know not . . . . Sometimes a man hits upon a place to which he mysteriously feels that he belongs. Here is the home he sought, and he will settle amid scenes that he has never seen before, among men he has never known, as though they were familiar to him from his birth."

To some it may seem peculiar, perhaps even indicative of emotional imbalance, that anyone could feel at home at the Coronet Hotel. They may well be right. The reason could be mysterious, as Maugham suggests, or possibly a clue can be found in one of Carol Hollinger's anecdotes about the university where she (and I) taught.

Many of her foreign associates—happy residents all—were of decidedly eccentric temperament, a fact noted with disapproval in certain staid embassy circles. Once a member of the latter group asked the Thai prince who headed the English department to explain this prevalence of *farang* oddities. The prince, so the story goes, suavely replied, "It is a prerequisite."

20

LIVING IN A MYTH

For a long time, to some extent still, accounts of real life murders held a strange fascination for me. *The Famous British Trials* series formed a treasured part of my book collection, and I could never read too many accounts of the mysterious events that took place on a hot August afternoon in Fall River, Massachusetts, toward the end of the nineteenth century, when Lizzie Borden may or may not have hacked her father and step-mother to death. Among the things that most intrigued me was the durability of many such cases and how subject they were to different interpretations from different perspectives. Even after more than a century, new books are still coming out about Lizzie Borden, that stern-faced spinster who stares so implacably at the camera in the photograph used in most, always, it seems, discovering some new angle, some fresh titbit of information overlooked or misinterpreted by earlier writers. I sometimes used to wonder idly what would it would be like to live not just at the same time and in the same place, but actually up close to a famous mystery, to observe the myth being shaped at first hand; and that is just what happened when my friend Jim Thompson disappeared in 1967.

"My friend Jim Thompson." The expression comes easily, but is it accurate? Were we really friends, did we really even like each other all that much? My proximity to the events surrounding his disappearance would remain the same in either case, but the relationship is perhaps one worth exploring in a little more detail than I have ever given it before.

Jim was the first person I met in Bangkok, when I came as a would-be writer of documentary film scripts. He was very hospitable. He cashed checks for me, invited me to dinner, got me a temporary membership in the Bangkok Sports Club. Most important of all, he introduced me to Charles Sheffield, his assistant at the Thai Silk Company, with whom I would spend thirteen years after I moved permanently to Thailand the next year. But Charles is the reason I question the friendship: I'm not sure Jim liked the idea of my moving in with Charles, certainly not in the beginning.

Here I must pause and wearily repeat a refrain I have often found necessary over the past thirty-odd years—Jim was *not* gay. Few are going to accept that just *because* I say it (a few, perhaps, are not going to because I say it), but it's true. Quite apart from the fact that he had a mistress, or at least a lady friend who was widely perceived to be that, I would have known if there were other interests; Bangkok was a small place in those days and there were not many secrets, especially about people as prominent as Jim. (We all knew about the gay ambassadors, the gay royals, the gay newspaper editors, the gay generals, the gay CIA agents.) In bringing it up here, I just want to emphasize that Jim's aversion to having me on the scene full-time was definitely not because of any such feelings he had toward Charles.

I think it may have had something to do with my personality. Charles was reserved, even dignified; whatever his private opinions (and these were often very different from what people thought), he seemed to play the role expected of him at Jim's gatherings. I, on the other hand, tended to bubble, to intrude on conversations, to pronounce opinions. Much more to the point, I was an outsider who was suddenly expected to be a part of what was a very small, very close-knit group that met daily for lunch at the club, several times a week for dinner, regularly at the silk company. As a visitor, I posed no threat, I would soon be gone; but as a permanent fixture, and particularly as somebody living with Charles, I had to be dealt with.

A., Jim's mistress, may have been partly responsible; another Frenchwoman who worked in the shop surely was. Both had a perhaps more than maternal affection for Charles and resented his taking up with someone they hardly knew and had never given their blessings to. (It was typical of Charles that he never told any of them I was coming, much less that I was going to share his house.) Thus without warning they were expected to make another place at the table, and they understandably resented it. I think they made this clear to Jim and that he probably took his lead from them.

I became aware of my changed status almost as soon as I came back to live. Along with Charles, I was asked to dinner during the first week, but then the invitations became rare. Charles would be asked alone, and since he had a specific function—a regular seat, as it were—he went. This was also typical of him, as I discovered; he was the reverse of demonstrative and was probably having his own problems getting adjusted to me, to the idea of living with anyone. Gradually, he and I worked out our difficulties, to the point where we evolved a lifestyle that gave each other ample private space. The relationship with Jim, A., and the other Frenchwoman proved more difficult and the sense of tension lasted for a long time. A. was the first to unbend; for all her notorious temper and rudeness, she was basically a kind-hearted woman, and once she realized I was there to stay she decided to look for my good points and make me welcome. Jim reached the same conclusion a little later, I think; the other woman held out for much longer and may still, without realizing it, harbour resentments against my intrusion nearly forty years ago.

By the time Charles and I moved into our second house, I had settled into a job of my own, with a circle of friends outside that regular group at the Sports Club and interests that ranged from writing to gardening. I was no longer dependent on them for my social life, was perhaps even a good influence on seemingly aloof Charles. Jim began dropping in to look at the garden, sometimes when Charles was abroad; he invited me alone to dinner a few times; I would go to see him at the Bangkok Nursing Home when he was suffering from one of his frequent illnesses. We saw each other particularly often when I helped make the arrangements with a Tokyo publisher for a new book he wanted to do on his house and collection and agreed to write the text for it.

But despite these changes, it never became a warm friendship. I always remembered those early months and he, I think, never quite felt comfortable with me. Separately we decided on a polite but some-what reserved relationship, based on Charles. Perhaps it was just as well that we never progressed beyond this point. Later it enabled me to stand back and see him a little more objectively than I might if I had regarded him really as a close friend.

Even then I found it hard to capture Jim's personality in words. He presented a curious mixture of openness and reserve, of kindness and something that could be close to cruelty. He reminded me in many ways of upper-class types I had known and disliked in New York, with ill-concealed prejudices and a tendency to pardon any lapse of good manners and intelligence in others of his class; and yet at the same time he had come so far beyond that world in his own life, had such an adventurous spirit about so many things. He was often very unkind to A., humiliating her in front of others, refusing to define the terms of their equivocal arrangement; yet he was immensely kind to near strangers and sensitive to their feelings. There was one man (was it significant that he was a friend of A.?) whose greatest social desire in the world was to attend just one dinner party at Jim Thompson's house; well aware of this, Jim never invited him, even with the groups of unknown tourists he often asked, and made his exclusion clear in many ways. (That man never forgot; years later, when my book on Jim came out, he wrote a savage review, mostly not about the book but about Jim's failings as a person.)

Perhaps it was simply that by the time I got to know him, Jim's shell of celebrity had hardened to the extent that few could penetrate it. Perhaps it was no longer possible for him to be totally relaxed and unaware of the impression he was making even in casual social contacts. Fame does that to people, I have noticed; they turn into the semifictional characters of the articles written about them, and no longer have any spontaneity or clear identity. It was easier with Jim, safer perhaps, to accept the surface and not attempt any greater intimacy.

But nevertheless he was a major part of our lives, the focus of many conversations as we walked around the garden with our afternoon drinks or sat on our landing over a *klong*; and so there was a feeling of genuine shock and loss when Charles came home that Monday afternoon in March of 1967 and said "Jim is missing". He had gone to the Cameron Highlands in Malaysia the previous week; we had been to his house just before his departure to get caption material for the book I was doing on the collection; there had been no omens, no sense of impending disaster. And yet here in the peaceful garden, about to embark on a daily routine: "Jim is missing."

What did "missing" mean? To us, of course, and I think to most people, it meant missing on one of the walks he was so fond of taking, perhaps collecting some plants for his own garden and ours. He must have strayed off a path in the jungle—Charles had been there on holiday and knew how wild it was—and had gotten lost. Even then I felt it might end in tragedy; by the time word had come to the silk company that morning, he had been missing for a whole night and half a day; but some kind of accident was all I could imagine by way of an explanation.

The next few days were nightmarish. As we had no telephone, Charles stayed either at the company or at our landlady's house, waiting for news. Jim's (and our) good friend Dr. Einer Ammundsen was in the Highlands, where he had gone to play golf, and he was the main source of information. Once the news appeared in the papers, sinister stories began making the rounds and at least one sinister visitor arrived at the gate one evening when I was home alone. It was an antique dealer who I'll call Emily Foo, notorious for smuggling out major works, and when I invited her to come in she shook her head and looked around nervously. "Just to let you know what happened to Thompson," she whispered. "Mangskau did it." The reference was to Connie Mangskau, a rival dealer who had gone to the Highlands with Jim, and the motive was obvious. "I'll pass on your information to Mr. Sheffield," I said, and she scurried off into the darkness.

I'm not sure just when I began to collect clippings about the case, but it was probably early on. The main reason at first was indignation; it amazed me that even reputable publications like the *New York Times* could get so many easily verified facts distorted or completely wrong. One of my first jobs had been on the *New Yorker* magazine, where I had been deeply impressed by the pains taken to check every fact, however small, that appeared in its pages, and I innocently supposed others had similar standards. The coverage of Jim's disappearance quickly shattered that illusion. From minor things like his exact age and birthplace to more serious ones like his holdings in the silk company and personal wealth, reporters blithely passed on gossip as fact and very seldom bothered to make a simple telephone call that would have clarified the matter.

In addition, there were all the bizarre things that were undeniably happening: mediums who went into trances and "saw" exactly where Jim was at the moment, foreign clairvoyants like Peter Hurkos (sent, in a moment of desperation, by Jim's family in America) who impressed a lot of supposedly intelligent people though his actual revelations were worthless, absurd theories that were espoused by other intelligent people over dinner tables, blending fact with fiction in a reckless way. Charles brought most of these stories home with him (including the details of a trip he himself made to Malaysia to check out a kidnapping allegation) and I began to make notes about these as well. We laughed at first over some of the wilder ones but stopped when we realized that they were actually being taken seriously.

Suddenly I realized that I was indeed living inside both a mystery and a rapidly accumulating myth—inside because although I was not playing a direct role in the production, I had a front row seat, easy access to everything going on backstage, personal knowledge of all the leading actors. Unlike outside reporters, I knew which stories to dismiss because of their sources and the sometimes subtle psychological pressures that were influencing certain of the actors. It was an odd sensation to be inside/outside, as I had suspected it might be, and before long I knew I had the basic ingredients of a story that could correct some of the more glaring errors about Jim and also express some of my own experiences of living and working in Thailand.

A year after the disappearance, I suggested an article to the *New York Times* Sunday magazine, for which I had written a couple of previous pieces. The idea was accepted, and the article appeared in 1968. One of its readers was Frank Dyckman, an old friend from my New York days who was then an executive of Houghton Mifflin, which had recently published a book about living in Bangkok called *Mai Pen Rai Means Never Mind*. Frank suggested expanding the article into a full-length book, an appealing prospect to me since I needed more space to develop some of the events in my now bulging file.

Things became a little complex for a few months. Elinor Douglas, Jim's favourite sister, was encouraging and offered to let me see some of the letters Jim had written her regularly over the years. Since Jim was still legally alive, however, and would remain so for another seven years, the letters were his possessions and had to be paraphrased rather than quoted directly. Then there was the murder of another sister, Katharine Wood, which many people (among them the ever-helpful Peter Hurkos) were trying to link with his disappearance; this, too, was never solved, and while I had reliable sources as to the murderer's identity (quite unrelated to Jim's case) I had to be very careful in discussing it. Finally, there was the problem of what to do about A. and at least one other love interest most of us in Bangkok knew about. A. was very much married to a prominent man, whose career might conceivably suffer if such information came out in cold print. I thus decided to mention her only in passing and leave out all discussion of Jim's private life, a decision that no doubt pleased the Thompson family but that led to much misinformed speculation later. (My mistake soon became evident. Within a year or so, other writers who never knew Jim were suggesting that he was a well-known homosexual on the apparent grounds that anyone with such artistic tastes had to be deviant, and a decade later this was widely accepted as "fact". Nor was A. happy: friends informed me that she was "furious" to find her great romance ignored and, living by then in Europe, she never wrote me a word about the book.)

But I had Charles' full cooperation and thus all the records of the Thai Silk Company, as well as intimate details of the search not available to outsiders. A number of the leading figures like Connie Mangskau, Dr. Ammundsen, Dr. and Mrs. Ling (owners of the bungalow where Jim was staying in the Highlands), and General Edwin Black (who had known Jim since his OSS days) were also good friends and willing to share their views with me. Thanks to these sources, as well as others back in the U.S., it was easy to assemble material and the book was fairly easy to write. (In passing, I might mention that the Jim remembered by his pre-war friends bore very little resemblance to the one I knew in Thailand.) If the final work had a point of view, it was less mine than that of Charles, who had a greater sense of honesty and propriety than almost anyone I have ever known: he would not have tolerated a sensational approach even if I had been tempted to take one.

Though like most authors I had dreams of instant glory, *The Legendary American*, as it was eventually called after many other titles had been rejected, had little effect in its original edition. It got good-enough reviews, though not in the places where it really counts; the first edition of 10,000 eventually sold out but there no second one in the U.S. by Houghton Mifflin. An obvious source of good sales was extremely difficult to find in those days. Bangkok had only one or two real bookshops, and they tended to order only three or possibly four copies at a time; since these came by sea, the time lapse was considerable. Eventually, though, a paperback edition was issued by John Weatherhill, a publisher in Tokyo, later another by the Thai Silk Company in Bangkok, and still later a revised edition by the Archipelago Press in Singapore. As a result, the book has remained more or less continuously in print for over thirty years, which if not exactly glory is no mean feat. I sold the movie rights to the Australian writer Morris West (author of *The Devils' Advocate*, *The Shoes of the Fisherman*, and other bestsellers), who at the time had a production company; nothing has ever developed out of this, though at one point I did meet a script writer in Los Angeles who had been hired to attempt a treatment. (Not to my surprise, it was the sensational possibilities that most interested him; I was polite but not, I fear, very helpful.)

So I discovered what it was like to be inside a famous case and to write about it. From a reporter's standpoint it was a rare opportunity, probably never to be repeated, but it also had its disillusioning side. Quite early on, someone told me he had read my book and was happy to find that I agreed with him about the solution. This was a surprise, partly because I thought I had been careful to present all the current theories without obviously favouring any of them and, even more, because I knew I disagreed strongly with the one he was said to hold. But as many other writers could probably have told me, people read what they want to read and firm opinions are rarely changed by seeing them refuted in print. As far as I know, all the facts I so carefully checked and assembled, all the false ideas I believed I had thoroughly discredited, had not the least effect on what people "knew" about Jim's life or what they thought happened to him that Easter Sunday afternoon. Just as Lizzie Borden has receded into misty myth, subject to as many interpretations as any Greek hero or heroine, so, it seems, will Jim Thompson. I have found it a sobering realization.

21

BANGKOK IN THE SIXTIES

A term much in vogue back in the fifties and sixties, especially in official American circles, was "culture shock", by which was meant the traumatic effect of moving suddenly from a familiar environment to one that was strange and, most likely, unsettling. Great difficulties, social and psychological, were alleged to result from such a move, and pamphlets were published offering advice on how to overcome or at least mitigate them. I only saw this material after I came to live in Bangkok in the summer of 1960 and was thankful to have been spared; had I read it before I might have taken it to heart and suffered from the dire complaint, as many others undoubtedly did.

My own change of environment could scarcely have been more total, starting with my first house. It was one that Jim Thompson had built on a piece of land he leased for ten years and that had been taken over in the seventh year by Charles Sheffield, his assistant at the Thai Silk Company, who in turn invited me to share it with him. (Jim timed it perfectly; on the day we moved, when the lease was up, one termite-riddled wall of the kitchen collapsed.) Today the site is occupied by part of a high-rise office building and part of a massage parlour, just a few feet from a perpetually jammed eight-lane avenue; but then it overlooked a *klong* shaded by huge rain trees thick enough to screen the open ground-floor rooms from the light traffic along Rama IV Road, with a small but luxuriant garden on three sides. There was a living room, dining room, and kitchen below and upstairs two bedrooms and a bath. Near the gate was a ramshackle former garage that had been converted into quarters for a cook, a houseboy, and a gardener—then regarded as the absolute minimum staff for even the most modest domestic establishment.

It was undeniably exotic, especially in the evening when lights softened by Chinese paper lanterns hid the exposed wiring and rather crude construction of the wooden walls (the whole structure, plumbing and all, had cost Jim less than $10,000) and moonlight glinted through the rain tree branches on the black waters of the *klong*. It also had certain drawbacks as far as creature comforts were concerned.

Dogs, cats, mosquitoes, lizards, and occasional snakes had free access to the ground floor rooms and took ample advantage of it, especially in the rainy season when the *klong* rose and sometimes flooded the garden. There was no telephone, no air conditioning, no hot water, and no gas; we cooked on a charcoal stove, and when the water supply failed (as it did regularly if two taps were turned on at the same time) we bathed with a dipper from a large jar, shouting *pit nam* ("close the water") to anyone who might be listening. Two or three times a week the electricity went off for several hours, nearly always at night; even when it worked the slightest overload, like turning on a spotlight to illuminate the garden, promptly blew all the fuses. The refrigerator, an ancient pre-war model, barely chilled; we bought blocks of ice daily and kept them in a large chest, along within any food likely to spoil soon. During the dry months, from November through May, the *klong* became a sinister trickle that smelt of sewage and dead things, floating a few yards from the dining room. Just beyond the back fence was a swampy, overgrown patch of wasteland; most of our mosquitoes and reptilian visitors came from there and so, late at night, did frequent banshee wails from an elderly drunken hag who had built a squatter shack in the shrubbery and who was said by the servants to be a witch.

All these features, or most of them, were by no means peculiar to our compound. They were common to most of Bangkok in those days, the topics of casual conversation at elegant dinner parties everywhere in the city: "Tell them about the cobra you found in the china closet, Diana." And strangely, none of them produced even a twinge of culture shock in my case. I discovered unexpected skills at changing old-fashioned fuses by candlelight in a thunderstorm, bathed every night in a nasty-smelling mosquito repellent called Sketolene, mastered the use of a charcoal oven (you put it over a fire and then piled hot coals on top to achieve an amazingly consistent temperature), and quickly learned to ignore the *klong* aromas. Only much later did I look back and marvel at how easy the adjustment had been.

It was the same with the city outside, which some people detested on sight but which fascinated me from the beginning. In the early sixties, Bangkok was a bewildering sprawl of low buildings, few of them taller than three or four stories, and visually not very attractive; dingy row shops lined most of the streets and the famous *klong* that inspire such nostalgia today had nearly all become like the one outside our house, basically open sewers periodically flushed by heavy rains. A noisy tram line still ran down the centre of dusty New Road, the principal shopping street for foreigners ("the meanest Main Street in Asia," one unkind observer called it), and pedicabs still wove a perilous path through a maze of smoke-belching buses and elderly Austin taxis. (Both tram and pedicab, however, were already on their way out; within a year of my arrival they had gone.) Earlier city planners were particularly fond of roundabouts (*wong wian*), which, given the driving habits of most Thai, created horrendous traffic problems and frequent accidents. The Grand Palace and the great Buddhist temples were splendidly exotic sights, of course, and the Chao Phraya River provided an always beguiling spectacle; but by and large the city's charms were hidden from public view, its appeal a matter of taste and serendipitous discovery.

The age of mass tourism was just beginning. Those who came often arrived on cruise ships in the spring, the worst time to visit Bangkok since it is the middle of the hot season but scheduled to coincide with the fabled cherry blossoms in Japan. Panting and perspiring, they anchored at the mouth of the river and came up in lighters, filled Jim Thompson's little silk shop on lower Suriwong Road for a few hectic hours, bought a few dubious stones from jewellery shops, did the obligatory temple tour, and then disappeared at sundown. Some were starting to come by air, though, driving into town through rice fields from Don Muang Airport and staying for longer periods in the few good hotels then available for them.

Most famous was the Oriental, a venerable, historic establishment but then a far cry from today's award-winning luxury. Lucky guests got a room in the new Tower Wing, built in 1958 and boasting some of Bangkok's first elevators; others, though, stayed in a long, low wing popularly known as "the bowling alley", where the amenities were much less up-to-date. Also popular was the Trocadero, just off New Road, which appealed to business travellers and journalists, and on the other side of town, near the Grand Palace, there was the Rattanakosin (the Rat, as everyone called it), a rather dreary place that somehow never caught on. But the hotel of the moment was the new Erawan, built by the government at great expense in an area not then regarded as fashionable or convenient; official guests were housed there and some others, like Somerset Maugham on his last trip, chose it because it was supposed to be the most modern. (We locals went often to the Erawan Tea Room, which had the best ice cream and cakes in town.)

I can't remember ever going to an apartment in the sixties, though I believe a few had been built. Everybody we knew lived in houses, big or small, simple or grand, always with servants and gardens. As only a few people had telephones at home, we either called each other at work or sent messages by one of the servants to arrange dinner parties. There were a great many of these, since Bangkok offered only a few respectable places where couples could go for an evening out, mostly either one of the hotels or big Chinese restaurants. Good, attractively-decorated Thai restaurants were non-existent; when asked why, Thai friends said the local cuisine could only be properly prepared at home and they preferred Chinese or Western when eating out so as to avoid disappointment. (They complained most bitterly, however, usually among themselves, when some *farang* offered them a home-cooked Thai meal; it was never quite right.)

A *farang* hostess with culinary aspirations but without access to one of the embassy resources had a difficult time. There were no supermarkets and only one or two shops that offered imported delicacies. The Silom Store was one, loyally supported by old-timers because it had supposedly sent food to foreigners who were interned at Thammasat University during the war; another, behind the National Lottery, was owned by a defrocked Italian priest with numerous small children who periodically placed a small advertisement in the *Bangkok Post* announcing CHEESE HAS ARRIVED. (I believe he sent out special announcements to a few select clients like the Oriental; by the time most of us got there, only a few mouldy specimens remained.)

Hostesses also had other, more specialized problems. The lights might go out during dinner, in which case candles had to be quickly organized, or the heavens might open in a flooding deluge. One enterprising lady I knew, who lived in a particularly low area, hired a fleet of pedicabs to transport her guests down the knee-deep lane and deposit them on her comparatively dry front steps.

The public markets, of course, were piled high with delectables used in local cooking, but there was not much variety for foreign tastes—string beans, mealy potatoes, cabbage, and cauliflower were the main vegetable staples, chicken and pork the most dependable meats; seafood required a good eye (and nose) since refrigeration was not very reliable. Cooks went to the market daily for these ingredients and, in many expatriate households, were expected to keep a careful account book listing how much had been spent on each. I started out doing this but quickly gave up; it seemed absurd when I had no idea what a kilo of potatoes was supposed to cost.

Shopping for other kinds of goods involved travel to various parts of the city, often quite far away. New Road was mainly for tourists but it did have a few good tailors and jewellery shops, as well as the British Dispensary, the place to go for medicines. For antiques we went to Nakorn Kasem, in the bowels of Chinatown, where you could find everything from a rare Ming bowl to a hand-operated ice cream machine; nearby was Pahurat, the Indian market, which sold imported textiles. Books were a real problem. Chalermnit in the Erawan Arcade offered a limited selection, rarely more than one or two copies of each, and Central Department Store, in Wang Burapha, sold paperbacks; but most of us who read had to satisfy our hunger by joining the private Neilson Hayes Library on Suriwong Road, which ordered most of the latest bestsellers and had a good reference section. Certain streets were devoted exclusively to office furniture, bathroom fixtures, and kitchen equipment, each lined with shops seemingly owned by members of the same family, charging the same prices. On Saturday and Sunday there was the great Weekend Market, then held at Sanam Luang across from the Grand Palace, where you could find just about anything if you had the stamina to search for it.

For single men—or, for that matter, married men out for an evening on their own—the opportunities for amusement were extensive, then as now. There were nightclubs where "dancing girls" could be hired, among them some upmarket places like the Sani Chateau and the Sala Thai, and others on the low side like a rowdy collection bearing such names as the Venus and the Mosquito Bar just across from the port at Klong Toey, where brawls were not infrequent. (Girls at the Mosquito Bar often wore costumes aimed at attracting what they believed to be the secret fantasies of their maritime clients; one, I remember, dressed regularly in a Japanese kimono, and a dwarf appeared demurely in a complete schoolgirl uniform.) In Chinatown, there were "tea shops" with rooms behind, as well as shophouses where grainy, locally-made dirty movies were shown, often in the family bedroom after grandparents and sleepy children had been shooed out. Along Rajadamnoen Avenue there were "day clubs" where men from nearby government offices went to amuse themselves at lunch time. Massage parlours were not, as some have suggested, invented for American GIs on R&R from Vietnam; there were plenty of them around in 1960, though not perhaps as opulent as the grand establishments that later rose.

Indeed, sex was a pervasive element of Bangkok life, however much some modern Thais like to pretend it was a Western introduction of recent vintage. When Somerset Maugham paid his first visit to the city in 1922, a street tout handed him a card offering the services of a certain "Miss Pretty Girl" who would massage him from "tippy toe to headtop" with perfumed soap. By the time I came, the cards were cruder and more concise ("Blow job, etc." one read in its entirety) but they were still being freely handed out by taxi drivers—one of them to an elderly foreign lady on her way to my house for dinner. That epic work *Emmanuelle* was composed in the mid-sixties (by a Frenchman married to a ravishing Thai girl) and according to those in the know, it was not based entirely on his imagination.

In this atmosphere, many *farang* marriages foundered. At the university where I worked we had a position informally known as "the Australian chair", occupied by a succession of women married to men at their embassy. Every one of these women was an outstanding beauty, charming and intelligent; every one of them lost her husband to one of the girls who worked at a bar that just happened to be just down the street from the embassy, popular as a place to stop in for a relaxing beer after the day's work.

More innocently, we could also find diversion through a few excursions out of town. Hua Hin, Thailand's oldest seaside resort, was a long drive on terrible roads and a bit somnolent when you got there, being mainly occupied by aristocratic Thais who had villas along the beach. More popular with younger foreigners was Pattaya, on the opposite side of the gulf, little more at the time than a fishing village with a few bungalows for rent, but the water was wonderfully clear and there was a semblance of night life in the form of a few good seafood restaurants. The more adventurous went to Chiang Mai by train (the highways were often impassable in the rainy season and bad at any time) and stayed at the Railway Hotel, a gloomy wooden structure just across from the station. Chiang Mai then was a leisurely little town that retired about nine o'clock, though noted for its exuberant festivals, handicrafts, and hospitable people, who routinely placed an earthen-ware jar of cool, fresh water outside their gates for the benefit of passing strangers. (You could also take an epic trip all the way from Chiang Mai to Bangkok by river on a bamboo raft, taking two weeks; that ended when the first dam was built.)

The foreign community in Bangkok was small—a handful of businessmen like Jim Thompson, plus some sent for tours of duty to head large organizations like the East Asiatic Company and the Hong Kong and Shanghai Bank; diplomats who largely entertained each other; a few doctors, most of them medical missionaries; a few lawyers; some international aid people, who were not really permanent since they changed frequently; spies, mostly attached to embassies but with curiously ill-defined duties; and a miscellaneous group that included English teachers, journalists, anthropologists, and others who had decided for a variety of personal reasons to settle down in Bangkok. A surprising number of these people knew each other, if only by sight or reputation, and often met at large receptions or national days.

Many belonged to the Royal Bangkok Sports Club, which had been established at the beginning of the century, largely at the instigation of resident Europeans though its membership had always included Thais (who now, of course, predominate). The club had a large swimming pool, squash and tennis courts, a small golf course (one of the first in Thailand) and a track for horses especially bred for racing in the tropics. The food was never very good (which is perhaps why the dining room was rarely used for parties), but the pool and golf course were popular—the pool in particular when the wife of the author of *Emmanuelle* appeared one memorable day in the first bikini ever to be seen in Bangkok. On racing weekends, when the public was admitted, the stands were packed and Rajadamri Road, which ran along one side of the course, was equally jammed with outside gamblers who followed the competition by signalling from strategic vantage points.

A week after arriving, I became a lecturer (an *acharn*) at Chulalongkorn University, or Chula as it was popularly known, and so entered a largely Thai world. Carol Hollinger, who taught there in the late fifties, perfectly captured the experience of a newcomer in *Mai Pen Rai Means Never Mind*: "In a first class not a soul understands a word you say. Since Siamese is a tonal language, I decided, after many brushes with this 'first class' phenomenon, that even those Thais most proficient in English must take a few minutes to adjust to the tone quality of a *farang's* voice. As soon as a new instructor finishes his first sentence all the students turn around and start screaming at each other in Siamese. The new teacher is overwhelmed by a sense of impending anarchy and thinks he has said something to infuriate them. Gradually, the excited students settle into a caucus, which clusters around the best English student in the class, in a frantic effort to find out what the *farang* has said. It is easy to wilt in this chaos. One short-lived *acharn* explained his failure angrily to me. 'They held *committee* meetings during my lecture!' he wailed."

Like Carol Hollinger, I adjusted to this, too, with surprising ease and went on teaching at the university for the next thirty years. It brought me into contact with a different society from that available to most expatriates and, I think, gave me a deeper, or at least more varied, understanding of the culture. It also introduced me to many of Bangkok's more eccentric *farang*, who for some reason seemed attracted to an academic career, perhaps because in those days credentials were not examined quite so scrupulously when a new teacher was urgently needed. (The atmosphere at Chula was amazingly relaxed. On my first day, when I was supposed to teach a freshman course called Civilization—prehistoric times to the atomic bomb, in thirteen concentrated hours—I inadvertently went to the wrong room and lectured to a class of bemused biology students, not one of whom uttered a word of complaint; the head of my department, a Thai prince who had gone to Cambridge, shrugged off the mistake as if it happened every day.)

As the sixties progressed, much of this atmosphere faded. In my second house, to which I moved in 1963, I had airconditioning, screens on all the windows, a gas stove, a brand-new refrigerator, reliable water and electricity (but still no telephone). Jim Thompson, who scorned such amenities for himself, disapproved; but I accepted them readily and soon wondered how I could ever have lived without them. I was on another *klong*, but it was one of the few that was still clean (at least in those days; no longer, alas) and offered such interesting sights as little floating brothels, each a *sampan* with a curtained area behind which a prostitute lolled on cushions, soliciting customers who waited beneath the bridges.

The first GIs from Vietnam arrived about the same time. Most were stationed upcountry at enormous air bases (the existence of which was solemnly denied at embassy press conferences), while others came on Rest and Recreation leave, two-week visits during which, for a remarkably low price, they got an airconditioned hotel room, a girl of their choice, and a selection of cultural and shopping tours. Though dozens, perhaps hundreds, of jerry-built hotels, shops, and bars rose to accommodate their needs, they affected the lives of the permanent *farang* community only slightly. The soldiers were forbidden to wear uniforms, for one thing (though it was easy to spot them on the streets), and for another, most of the bars were in areas we did not often frequent. Spared the nightly television coverage that made such an impact on American homes, we knew little more of what was going on in Saigon than what we learned from reports in the *Bangkok Post* and the *Bangkok World*. (My mother, whose knowledge of Southeast Asian geography was hazy, would send me frantic letters every time there was a major disaster, like the Tet offensive, wanting to know if I needed an urgent ticket to get home.)

Nor did most of us take any interest in Thai politics. The military seemed firmly in control, supported by the American government, and any changes were mostly cosmetic. There were a couple of coups, but they were always bloodless and often internal—the point usually seemed to be to throw out whatever constitution was in effect and start writing another—and they always took place on the other side of town; the first we learned of them was an announcement on the radio or in the papers the next morning.

Other changes were more visible or personal. The *klong* began to disappear to make room for wider streets, until there were hardly any left in Bangkok proper. The one I lived on survived, but the floating brothels and little canoes gave way to long-tailed motorboats that roared past like jet planes and soon led to permanent pollution.

Buildings got taller (though not much more attractive). The centre of things gradually moved away from New Road and the river. The girls at the university started wearing short skirts instead of the old ones that almost touched the ground, and the boys started wearing Beatle-style haircuts and skin-tight trousers; they started complaining, too, about the iniquities of the military government and singing the protest songs then so popular on American campuses, though the first real demonstrations (and the first blood) would not come until the seventies.

A proper Japanese-owned department store opened at the end of the decade, and a real supermarket. Television arrived, with all that it implied. Tourists began to come, many of them people who would not have dreamed of leaving their home countries only a few years before. More to cater to their tastes than to the GIs, Patpong Road was transformed from a rather ordinary street of travel agents and restaurants into a neon-lit maze of bars with go-go girls and shows of astonishing variety. Jim Thompson mysteriously disappeared while on a holiday in Malaysia (shortly after he had moved his little silk shop to a far grander one at the other end of Suriwong Road), and Darrell Berrigan, a friend who edited the *Bangkok World*, was brutally murdered.

But I don't think I really realized that so much of the Bangkok I first knew had gone until the early seventies, when a visiting reporter asked if he could interview me. Though I had for some time ceased to be the designated newcomer in my crowd, the one to whom people said "You should have been here when . . . ", I was still discovering new aspects of the city and still constantly amazed by its variety. I was thus non-plussed when the reporter announced the subject of the interview as "the ancient days".

"You mean Ayutthaya?" I asked, wondering why he had assumed I was an expert on history.

"No," he said, turning on his tape recorder. "I want to know what Bangkok was like ten years ago."